Introduction

Many young people who embark on careers in entertainment were inspired by performers who came before them. They saw a famous singer sing, an actor act, a dancer dance, and thought, *Wow, I want to be like them someday!*

But for others, there was nobody ahead that looked like them, thought like them, or talked about experiences they shared. Without examples to follow, what could these young dreamers do? Well, the exceptional people in this book refused to be discouraged. Instead, they forged their own path. They declared, “We belong. We can perform, model, direct, produce, and write. We do it all in our unique way.”

Thank goodness these historically marginalized voices prevailed, because for years, people were shut out of certain spaces because of their race, gender, disabilities, religion, sexuality, or body type. The entertainment industry needed change. The talented individuals in this book met that challenge and found a way to make their voices heard. They fought through bias and barriers while opening doors and minds along the way. It wasn’t easy, and it didn’t happen overnight, but the journey was important.

Look at Misty Copeland (page 20), who was the first Black female principal dancer at the American Ballet Theatre in New York City. She showed the world that ballet “can be and should be inclusive.” Today, little Black girls look up to Misty and think, *I can be like her!* Model Ashley Graham (page 38) proved that beauty has nothing to do with a person’s size. Chris Burke (page 12), the first TV star with Down syndrome, brought welcome diversity to the small screen. James Wong Howe (page 48), who became the first Asian person to win an Oscar in 1955, blazed the trail for other Asian Americans in the film industry. Thanks to all these stars and others, the world of entertainment is now filled with more diversity on the stage, behind the camera, on the runway, and on the screen. Who was the first deaf actor to win an Oscar? Who was the first transgender person to be nominated for an Emmy Award? How about the first Black person to win the Caldecott Medal for best illustrated children’s book? How many women have broken through entertainment barriers to make their mark? The answers to these questions are all found in the following pages.

This book is a celebration of the awesome achievements of all these innovators. The world is a diverse place, and the entertainment world is becoming that way too. Of course, there is still more work to be done, but the trailblazers in this book inspire current and future generations to challenge boundaries through determination, hard work, and talent. One day, even more artists and performers—from actors and musicians to writers and photographers—will leave their mark on the world and make the entertainment industry a more welcoming space for all. Lights! Camera! Inclusion!

A Century of Firsts

Today's world of entertainment holds a dizzying set of choices—from movies in theaters or online, from TV channels or streaming shows, from your phone or your tablet, on stages big or small. American entertainment has grown enormously in the twentieth and twenty-first centuries. Before we celebrate the fearless individuals who helped create that growth, here's a look at a timeline of key firsts in events that helped these amazing entertainers reach their fans!

1901
First Nobel Prize in Literature: France's Sully Prudhomme

1896
First movie theater in the United States

1918
First Pulitzer Prize for Fiction: American writer Ernest Poole

1920
First radio station: KDKA in Pittsburgh

1926
First national TV network: NBC

1927
First movie with sound: *The Jazz Singer*

1929
First Academy Awards (for film) ceremony

1947
First Tony Awards (for theater) ceremony

Fun fact: The Tonys are the only major awards officially named for a person. Winners receive the Antoinette Perry Award for Excellence in Theatre. "Tony" was Antoinette's nickname; she was a 1920s actor and director.

1949
First Emmy Awards (for TV) ceremony

FEARLESS FIRSTS

ARTISTS WHO CHANGED ENTERTAINMENT

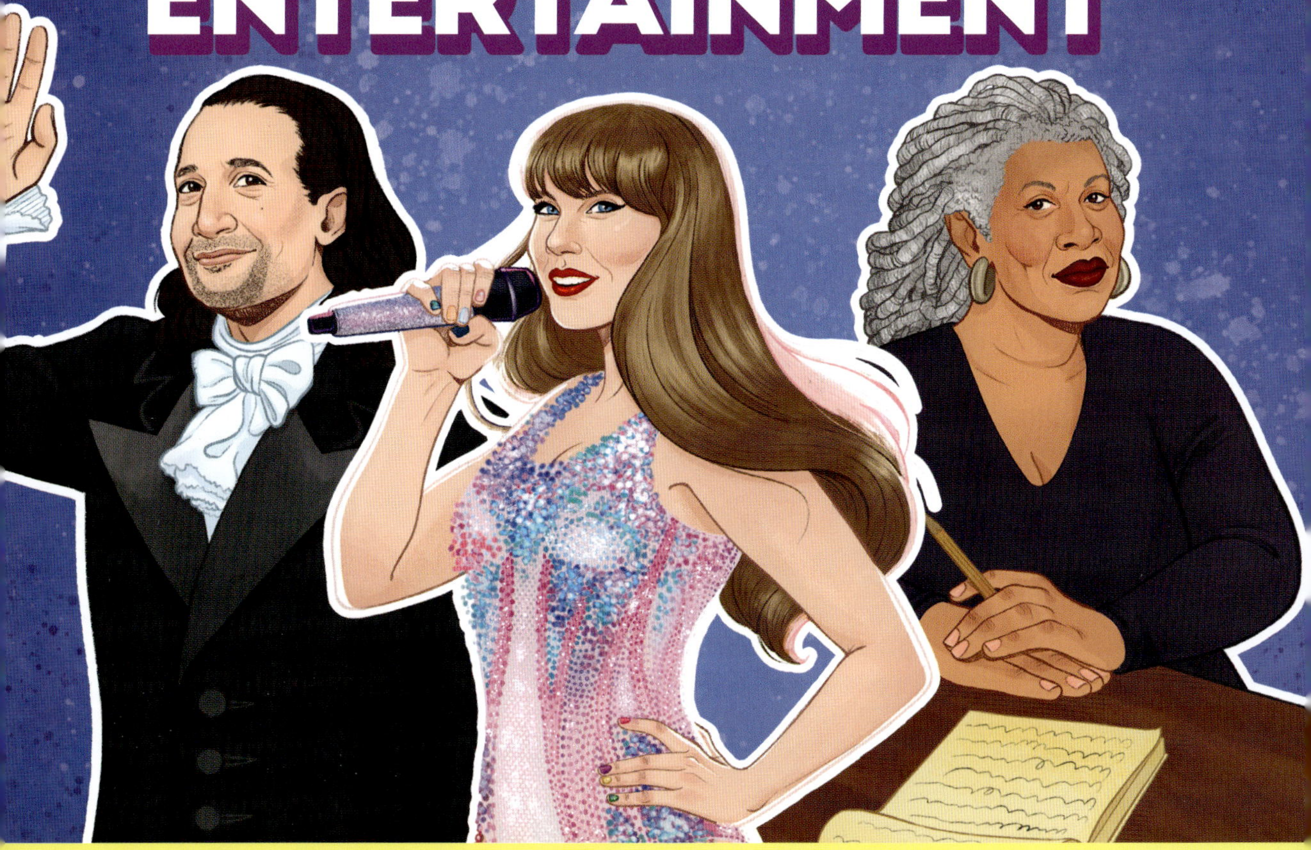

WRITTEN BY
JAMES BUCKLEY JR. & ELLEN LABRECQUE

PICTURES BY
STEFFI WALTHALL

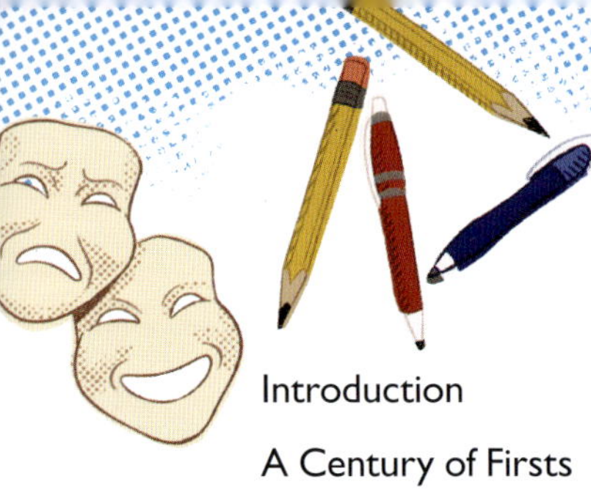

Table of Contents

1958
First Grammy Awards (for music) ceremony

1980
First video game character: Pac-Man

1984
Telemundo founded

1992
First music website: Cybergrass, featuring bluegrass music

1993
First movie website: IMDb

2001
First BET Awards

2005
First online streaming service: YouTube

2014
First TikTok post

A Letter to Parents

Dear parents and guardians,

We hope your children enjoy reading about these fearless firsts in the entertainment industry as much as we enjoyed writing about them. We also hope these remarkable accomplishments captivate your children and persuade them to follow their own goals and dreams.

We acknowledge that some of the films and television shows mentioned in these pages contain mature content. We also know that you, as parents, play a vital role in guiding the media choices of your children. With this understanding, we have included official ratings (PG-13 or TV-14 and higher) whenever possible. We hope these serve as a tool for you to help make informed decisions.

As your kids grow older, we hope they eventually revisit these stories with an even deeper understanding and appreciation of the people and performances included.

Thank you for taking the time to nurture your child's media choices. Most of all, thank you for raising exceptional and wonderful readers!

Mahershala Ali

First Muslim Actor to Win an Oscar

BORN 1974

When Mahershala Ali's name was announced as the 2017 Oscar winner for Best Actor in a Supporting Role, the Hollywood audience of artists and celebrities gave him a standing ovation. Leading up to the event, the Academy of Motion Picture Arts and Sciences, the organization that presents the Oscars, had been heavily criticized for failing to recognize actors and artists from diverse backgrounds. For instance, in 2015 and 2016, all twenty actor nominations went to white actors. As a result, the hashtag #OscarsSoWhite had gone viral on social media.

When Mahershala won for his role in *Moonlight* (R), he became the first Muslim actor to win an Oscar. Just one year later, Mahershala won his second Oscar for his supporting role in the movie *Green Book* (PG-13). This made him the first Black actor to win two Academy Awards in the same category.

Mahershala was born Mahershalalhashbaz Gilmore in Oakland, California, and was raised Christian. He grew up playing basketball and earned a sports scholarship to Saint Mary's College in California. Even though he was there to play hoops, Mahershala discovered his love for acting and joined the cast of the school plays. After college in the late 1990s, he went to graduate school to study acting at New York University. While in New York, he converted to Islam and changed his last name to Ali.

"There was this connection that pierced through it all for me," he said about joining the Muslim community. "I felt like I was in the right place."

Throughout his life, Mahershala first faced discrimination as a Black man and then as a Black Muslim man. When he shopped in department stores, salespeople followed him around because they thought he would steal something because of the color of his skin. And when he traveled, he was subjected to extra screening from airport security because of his Muslim name.

Mahershala spoke out about the importance of acceptance. He explained there is the opportunity to embrace differences, to see "the texture of a person and what makes them unique." Now that Mahershala is one of the biggest movie stars in the world, acting in many award-winning films and popular true-life stories like *Hidden Figures*, he has even more opportunities to speak out against discrimination against Muslim people.

"We all need to do a better job," he said passionately at the end of one of his acceptance speeches.

Marian Anderson

First Black Singer to Perform at the Lincoln Memorial

1897–1993

How can racism create silence? By preventing one of the greatest singers of all time, Marian Anderson, from taking the stage. By the time Marian was in her twenties in the early 1900s, she was one of the world's great contraltos. She had sold out concerts throughout Europe in front of enraptured fans. But in the United States, she was prevented from performing in certain places because she was Black. Despite this discrimination, Marian kept singing.

Marian grew up in churches in Philadelphia, singing in choirs as her vocal talents began to soar. She trained with an opera teacher and won a contest in 1925 that kicked off her career, including an appearance that made her the first Black singer to perform with the New York Philharmonic Orchestra. She went on concert tours in the southern and eastern states, usually playing to all-Black audiences because many theaters did not allow Black performers. To find bigger crowds, Marian moved to Europe. Audiences there were thrilled, and she spent most of the 1930s touring in front of royalty and filling auditoriums in London, Stockholm, Copenhagen, and more.

In 1939, Marian tried to put on a concert in Washington, DC, but the theater manager refused because of her race. When this news got out, many fans were outraged, including Eleanor Roosevelt, wife of President Franklin Roosevelt. She helped arrange a free concert at the Lincoln Memorial, making Marian the first Black person (male or female) to perform there. More than seventy-five thousand attendees of all backgrounds were entranced by Marian's singing; millions more listened on the radio.

After World War II, Marian became the first Black singer to lead a performance at the Metropolitan Opera in New York City, where she played a witch named Ulrica in an Italian opera called *The Masked Ball*. As she continued to tour, she insisted all theaters where she performed be fully integrated.

In 1957, Marian's talent and her belief in the unifying power of music led to her becoming a goodwill ambassador for the U.S. In 1961, she sang at the inauguration of President John F. Kennedy and returned to the Lincoln Memorial in 1963 to perform during the March for Jobs and Freedom led by Dr. Martin Luther King Jr.

Marian received many honors in her life, including the Presidential Medal of Freedom in 1963 and the Grammy Lifetime Achievement Award in 1991. She became a national hero.

AAT
NBC
NBC

Desi Arnaz and Lucille Ball

First Latino and First Female TV Producers

DESI: 1917–1986, LUCILLE: 1911–1989

One of the most famous couples in TV history was also a titanic team of fearless firsts. Desi Arnaz and Lucille Ball were pioneers on and off the screen.

Desi Arnaz was born in Cuba. His family moved to Miami in the 1930s, and as a singer and bandleader, he helped make Cuban and Latin music popular in the United States. In 1940, Desi was in a movie called *Too Many Girls*, where he met and married a young actor named Lucille Ball. She had appeared in dozens of movies, singing, dancing, and showing a unique talent for comedy. Lucille became a big star in the 1940s, and Desi continued touring with his band.

Desi's outgoing personality led to his first "first." He hosted the 1950 TV game show *Your Tropical Trip*, which made him the first Latino to star in his own program. TV networks also wanted Lucille to do a show, but she would only do it if Desi could be her costar. Together, they created *I Love Lucy*, about a Cuban bandleader and his wife.

The show's first episode went on the air on October 15, 1951, and became a huge hit. It ran for seven years and remains one of TV's most popular comedies of all time.

I Love Lucy was pioneering in other ways. As producer of the show, Desi was the first to use a live audience for a TV comedy and the first to have three cameras filming at once. Hundreds of TV comedies have been done that way since. The show was also the first to be shown as reruns. Finally, *I Love Lucy* was one of the first shows made in Hollywood. At the time, most TV shows were filmed in New York City, but Desi and Lucille lived in Los Angeles, so they made sure the show was filmed near them instead.

Desi and Lucille also teamed up in the business world, creating Desilu Productions to make shows, including *The Andy Griffith Show* and *The Dick Van Dyke Show*.

The couple divorced in 1960 but remained friends and business partners for a time. In 1962, Desi left the company, and Lucille became the first woman to be president of a TV studio! Under Lucille's creative leadership, Desilu made hits out of the *Star Trek* and *Mission: Impossible* franchises.

Desi and Lucille transformed television in America. Every sitcom and every rerun you watch can be traced to these small-screen pioneers.

Ashley Boone Jr.

First Black President at a Major American Movie Studio

1938–1994

Are you a *Star Wars* fan? If so, you can thank Ashley Boone Jr. for making sure you got a chance to see those movies.

Ashley grew up in Massachusetts. He studied finance but chose to work in the movie business in New York City and Hollywood instead. Even early in his career, he proved he could "sell" movies. That is, he was skilled at making sure new movies attracted big audiences. This part of the movie business is called marketing, and Ashley became a master. One of his first successes was a movie called *Sounder*, based on a well-known book about a Black family and their dog; it was nominated for a Best Picture Oscar.

In 1977, a filmmaker named George Lucas brought a movie to 20th Century Fox Studios, where Ashley worked. He was one of the first people to see the film, and he knew it would be a hit. Ashley created a plan to get the movie out to millions of people quickly, an unusual move at the time. Ashley's plan worked, and that movie, *Star Wars*, became one of the biggest hits of all time. Lucas later credited Ashley and his team for making the *Star Wars* dream come true.

In 1979, Ashley was made president of marketing for 20th Century Fox, the first time a Black person had that job. He faced obstacles because of his race, like some staff not believing he was the boss, not being recognized for his work, or being forced to show ID when visiting other studios.

Unfortunately, Ashley was out of that job four months later—Hollywood jobs sometimes don't last long. So he created a new company that helped Lucas market the next *Star Wars* movies and went on to be president of marketing at several other studios. He promoted *Chariots of Fire*, *Ghostbusters*, *The Right Stuff*, and many other huge hits.

Sadly, Ashley died in 1994 of cancer at the age of fifty-five. But his sister, Cheryl Boone Isaacs, had followed him into the movie business. In 2013, she became the first Black person and first woman to be president of the Academy of Motion Picture Arts and Sciences.

Today, there are still only a handful of Black people in senior positions at big studios. They all look to Ashley as an example. His place in history was set, and the Force was with him!

DIRECTOR
DIRECTOR OF PHOTOGRAPHY
PROD. NO.
CAMERA NO.
DATE

Chris Burke

First Actor with Down Syndrome to Star in a TV Show

BORN 1965

In 2023, nearly one in seven hundred babies were born with Down syndrome. People born with this condition often have bodies and brains that work differently from other people's. Over time as a society, we have learned more about intellectual disabilities, including Down syndrome, and the importance of people with disabilities being fully included in society. Some of the shift in this understanding came after 1989 when actor Chris Burke became the first person with Down syndrome to star on TV.

"Back in those days, a parent looked at the disability and didn't see the ability," Chris remembered years after the show ended. "*Life Goes On* showed that people with a disability can be included. Just give them a chance and let them learn. That's what the show was trying to teach."

Chris grew up in New York City, where his siblings did some acting and modeling. By the time he was a teenager, Chris decided to become an actor too. This was a big step, since memorizing lines and speaking very clearly is a big part of most acting, but these skills can be difficult for people with Down syndrome. Still, Chris stuck with it and earned a few small roles. A TV producer saw one of them and decided to make a show that could feature Chris. *Life Goes On* debuted in 1989 with Chris as its groundbreaking star.

In the show, Chris played Corky Thatcher, who he called "an ordinary person who does extraordinary things. He is a true inspiration, but he doesn't know that he's an inspiration." The show focused on the family's choice to put Corky in a school with children who did not have the same challenges he did. It was a popular family show that earned good ratings and, more importantly, a lot of positive attention for people with Down syndrome.

The show ended in 1993, but Chris's impact has continued. For years, Chris has been an inspirational speaker and spokesperson for the National Down Syndrome Society. He has appeared as a guest star in other TV shows, and he tours as a singer with a folk band. Chris was among the many people who helped society realize that everyone has gifts to share, no matter what limitations they might have.

Patricia Cardoso

First Latina Director in National Film Registry

BORN 1961

Women star in movies all the time. However, most of those movies are directed by men. Some studies show that less than five percent of major studio movies are directed by women, and thus many in the business have recently started to call on more women to direct. In 2019, the skill of one of those directors was recognized when Patricia Cardoso's film *Real Women Have Curves* (PG-13) was added to the Library of Congress National Film Registry. It was the first time a Latina director's work was given this important honor.

"For me, being one of the first Latinx woman directors is very important," Patricia said after the registry announcement was made. "But I would wish I wasn't the first one. I wish there were many, many more before me and certainly hope there are many more coming behind me."

Directors following Patricia's example can look to her story with hope. Born in Colombia, she earned a degree in anthropology and then won a Fulbright scholarship to study film at UCLA. She spent about a decade making short films and working on other productions.

In 2002, she directed *Real Women*, which was based on a play written in 1990 by Mexican American playwright Josefina López. The story is about a young woman, played in the film by actor America Ferrara, as she struggles to choose between her family and her dreams of college. The movie features a cast of Latine actors and includes a storyline about body-image issues. *Real Women* won important awards, including the Audience Award at the famous Sundance Film Festival in Utah.

"It's so important for our community to grow up seeing images of people like them—to have role models," Patricia said later. "It's so detrimental to not see yourself with dignity and respect."

Sadly, Patricia herself faced the same barriers. Even after *Real Women* was finished, she struggled to get other movies made. For more than fifteen years, she worked various jobs, some of them outside the film or TV industry. It was not until 2019 that she got work directing again. That was also the year that *Real Women* earned its National Film Registry honor. Patricia has since worked on several TV movies, has other projects on her plate, and inspires future directors as a professor at the University of California, Riverside. In 2024, she became the first Latina elected to the director's section of the Board of Governors of the Academy of Motion Picture Arts and Sciences. She continues to work to create representation both on- and off-screen.

Ruth E. Carter

First Black Female Oscar Winner for Costume Design

BORN 1960

How do you make words on a page come to life in the movies? That's the skill of costume designers, who translate the words of a script into sketches and then into clothing worn by actors. For the 2019 movie *Black Panther* (PG-13), the visual genius behind the characters' outfits was Ruth E. Carter, whose work on the movie made her the first Black woman to win an Oscar for costume design.

Ruth grew up in Massachusetts. She learned to sew from her mother and enjoyed drawing and making art with her brothers. She got her first taste of costume design at a small theater in her hometown of Springfield while in high school and college. In 1986, Ruth moved to Los Angeles, where she connected with director Spike Lee. By the 1990s, she was working on new movies every year for Lee and others, designing both modern and historical costumes. That meant doing a lot of research and making sure her work was both beautiful and authentic.

Ruth's big win for *Black Panther* was not her first visit to Oscar night. She earned nominations in 1992 and 1997 for her costume designs in films about Black history. In her career so far, Ruth has created costumes for more than sixty movies.

For *Black Panther*, even though the film's setting of Wakanda was fictional, Ruth wanted the costumes to be connected to true African style. She was inspired by designs from people throughout the continent, including Zulu, Tuareg, Dogan, Turkana, and more. To create the more than seven hundred costumes for the film, she generated ideas from the original comics while adding her own flair for smoother movement. Star Chadwick Boseman specifically asked for a superhero costume in which he could leap, jump, and spin easily!

The movie was a huge hit, and Ruth's Wakanda look was a big part of the reason. In 2022, Ruth designed more than two thousand costumes for the sequel, *Wakanda Forever* (PG-13).

After winning the Oscar, Ruth acknowledged how much this might mean to future designers of color. "Finally, the door is wide open, and I've been struggling and digging deep and mentoring and doing whatever I could to raise others up," she said. "And I hope through my example, this means that there is hope and other people can come on in and win an Oscar just like I did."

Wakanda—and Ruth Carter—forever!

Nat King Cole

First Black Man to Host a TV Series

1919–1965

In late 1956, Nat King Cole, the famous singer and piano player, became the first Black man to host his own television show. *The Nat King Cole Show* featured talented musicians and actors—both Black and white—who performed skits and songs with Nat.

"I was the pioneer, the test case," Nat said. "On my show rode the hopes and fears and dreams of millions of people."

Nat was born Nathaniel Adams Coles in Montgomery, Alabama. His father was a preacher, and his mother played the organ in the church choir. Nat's mother taught her son how to play the piano by the time he was four years old. When Nat was still young, his family moved to Chicago, a city filled with a thriving jazz scene. Nat put together his own band in high school and made his first recording on piano at age seventeen. He also dropped the *s* from his last name and added King as his middle name.

After high school, Nat became the lead singer and piano player for a group called the King Cole Trio, which performed in Los Angeles. A music producer found them and helped them land a record contract with Capitol Records. The King Cole Trio recorded many number one hit songs, and because Nat was the lead singer, he became the most famous.

When Nat was offered his own television show in 1956, he was already one of the most popular entertainers in the country. His show immediately became a hit. But for the show to make money, it needed to get national advertisers, and such companies would not advertise on the show because Nat was Black. They were afraid if they did, white people would no longer buy their products, especially in the South. "Advertisers still think it's a white man's world," Nat said at the time.

Nat's show lasted only fourteen months, but it paved the way for future Black stars. Nat was the first to cross the color barrier on the television screen, and he crossed it in other ways too. He and his wife and children were the first Black family to buy a house in an all-white Los Angeles neighborhood.

One of Nat's most popular songs was "Unforgettable," where he sings, "Unforgettable in every way, and forevermore that's how you'll stay." The ballad is just like Nat King Cole himself—lasting and unforgettable.

Misty Copeland

First Black Female Principal Dancer at the American Ballet Theatre

BORN 1982

Misty Copeland envisions the world of ballet filled with dancers of different races, ethnicities, and body types. "It's so important to show people that ballet should be, and can be, inclusive," said Misty, and she was one of the first people to help make this a reality.

In 2015, at age thirty-three, Misty became the first Black female principal dancer at the American Ballet Theatre. A principal dancer holds the highest rank in the company, dancing the lead roles in the performances. "I'd done it. For myself and for all the little brown girls," Misty wrote in her autobiography, *Life in Motion*.

Misty was born in Kansas City, Missouri, but moved to San Pedro, California, when she was young. She and her five siblings were raised by their single mother. Misty was first introduced to ballet at a local Boys and Girls Club when she was thirteen. Most professional ballet dancers start dancing much earlier than this. Ballet dancers also usually have thin body types, but Misty's body is curvy, powerful, and athletic. Despite these differences, the teacher at the Boys and Girls Club spotted Misty's talent instantly. Misty was a natural dancer who wanted to be the best.

Just two years after Misty first began performing, she became one of the top ballet dancers in California. Two years after that, when Misty was seventeen, she auditioned to join the American Ballet Theatre, which offered her a full scholarship to perform with them in New York. When she joined, she became the only Black dancer in the company. Misty was extremely proud of this role, but she also felt isolated and different because of the color of her skin, her body type, and the number of years she'd been dancing. "I felt like I was sinking for a while," Misty admitted. "I felt alone in a world that had become my home."

Misty soon made it her life's mission to make the ballet space more diverse so no other dancer has to feel like an outsider the way she did. In 2022, Misty began a program called Be Bold. The program offers free ballet lessons for students of color at Boys and Girls Clubs in New York City, the same organization where she got her chance in California years earlier.

"I think that's my purpose," explained Misty, "to bring people in, to make them feel that they belong."

Laverne Cox

First Transgender Person to be Nominated for an Emmy

BORN 1972

Actor Laverne Cox was bullied as a child—"majorly bullied," she said. Growing up in Mobile, Alabama, Laverne was called names, chased by other kids, and even beaten up. Laverne was assigned male at birth, but she said, "I just thought I was a girl... In my imagination, I would hit puberty and start turning into a girl."

In sixth grade, the bullying got so bad that Laverne couldn't take it anymore. She wasn't sure she wanted to go on and considered ending it all. Thankfully, she didn't.

To make her life a little easier, Laverne did something she was passionate about and began taking dance lessons. She attended the Alabama School of Fine Arts for high school and later studied dance at Marymount Manhattan College in New York City. Laverne fell in love with acting and began living openly as a woman, taking hormone therapy and having gender-affirming surgery.

After graduating college, Laverne worked to become a professional actor. She earned small parts on television shows and in movies. In 2012, at age forty, she got her big break, landing the part of Sophia Burset, a transgender woman on the television show *Orange Is the New Black* (TV-MA). For this role, Laverne became the first openly transgender person to be nominated for an Emmy Award, television's highest honor. A year later, she became the first openly transgender woman to win a Daytime Emmy Award for her role as a producer for the show *Laverne Cox Presents: The T Word.*

Once Laverne became a television star, she opened doors for other transgender people, especially trans women of color, to bring their stories into the spotlight through TV, movies, and other media. She educates people about the trans community, their struggles, and how to make their lives better.

Laverne speaks at conferences and on television about how discrimination makes it hard for trans people to find jobs and safe places to live. She talks about how trans people are often victims of violence and hate crimes, bringing awareness to the issues to make a better world for herself and others.

"I feel compelled to try and educate as much as possible," Laverne said. "I feel compelled because there's so much injustice."

More than anything else, Laverne wants to help others who are like her. Since she was bullied as a child, she works tirelessly to stop this from happening to other trans youth.

Peter Dinklage

First Little Person to Win an Emmy

BORN 1969

Stereotyping means believing that everyone in a certain group is the same instead of treating each person in that group as an individual. For actors who are little people, that means they are often given stereotyped roles—as clowns, elves, or leprechauns. Peter Dinklage refused to take such parts and became a star in his own right. In 2011, he became the first little person to win an Emmy.

Peter was born in New Jersey with a condition called achondroplasia (uh-KON-droh-PLAY-zee-ah), a form of dwarfism. He caught the acting bug in grade school, when he realized he enjoyed hearing people clap for his performances. Peter acted throughout high school and college and then moved to New York City. His first work was in the theater; he even started an acting troupe with a friend. From his earliest days as an actor, Peter refused to take any roles that stereotyped little people, instead performing in Shakespeare's plays and other important works.

Peter's career has included characters in *Elf*, *Lassie*, *The Chronicles of Narnia*, *X-Men* (PG-13), and *The Avengers* (PG-13). He's also done some voice acting, including in the *Ice Age* films, the *Angry Birds* films, and *The Croods*. Peter's most famous role among adult TV viewers came in the television series *Game of Thrones* (TV-MA). His character was a fan favorite, and in 2011, Peter won the first of his four Emmy Awards for the show. By 2022, he had received nine nominations, including one as a producer.

Even as he has become a very popular TV and movie star, Peter has continued to speak out against stereotyping. In 2022, he criticized the planned Disney remake of *Snow White*, asking why studios thought it was still okay to do a movie focused on cartoon dwarves. However, Peter is also quick to say that he does not want to stereotype anyone himself.

"Everyone's different. Every person my size has a different life, a different history," he said. "[We have] different ways of dealing with it. Just because I'm seemingly okay with it, I can't preach how to be okay with it."

One thing everyone is okay with—Peter Dinklage continuing to act and stand for what he believes!

East West Players

First Asian American Theater Company

FOUNDED 1965

For many decades in Hollywood, most Asian characters in movies were stereotypes. They were villains with exaggerated accents or servants who bowed all the time. Even when parts for Asian characters were written, they were often played by white actors wearing makeup and using bad accents. It was offensive, but no one who objected was listened to. Through it all, Asian American actors kept plugging away, fighting for the right to play those parts and to tell their own stories.

In 1965, a group of those actors came together in Los Angeles to form East West Players, the first Asian American theater company. The group has put on hundreds of plays, inspiring actors, playwrights, and theater people of all backgrounds.

Theater has a long tradition in many Asian cultures. People who came to the United States from China and Japan, for instance, brought those styles of performance with them. However, they did not have many ways to showcase them, or if they did, it was for Asian audiences only. Also, anti-immigrant feelings in the United States made it hard for Asian actors to find a way forward.

Two forces came together to help create the East West Players. First, after World War II, there was a boom in small regional theater companies. Second, the Civil Rights Movement encouraged many ethnic communities to work for better representation.

Actors James Hong and Mako Iwamatsu were successful Asian American actors of this time, and they gathered other professionals, including Beulah Quo, Soon-tek Oh, Guy Lee, and Yet Lock, to form East West Players. While James was hoping to gain more movie roles through the company, Mako and others focused on training for the stage. The group's first show was *Rashomon*, based on a Japanese epic. The East West Players drew on Asian traditions while also performing shows outside of their heritage.

As the group grew in size and importance, East West became a rallying point for the larger Asian American community. They took the lead on social justice movements, such as when Asian American women were attacked in Atlanta in 2021.

Things for Asian American actors are better than they were, but much work still needs to be done. "When East West Players started, there was no one else doing what we're doing, and even now, locally and nationally, there are very few places," said East West artistic director Snehal Desai in 2022. Actor, director, and writer Lily Tung Crystal took over as artistic director in 2024.

Nobu McCarthy
James Hong
Lauren Tom
Snehal Desai
Soon Tek-Oh
Belulah Quo
Mako Iwamatsu
Dante Basco

Billie Eilish

First Pop Star Open about Living with Tourette Syndrome

BORN 2001

Singer-songwriter Billie Eilish has nothing to hide—especially when it comes to living with Tourette syndrome (TS). TS is when your brain makes your body move or say something that you don't want to do or say. These are called tics. The tics can be motor, like eye blinking, head shaking, and sudden movements, or they can be vocal, like coughing or throat clearing. Billie was diagnosed with TS when she was only eleven years old.

Billie says her tics are mainly physical; she wiggles her ears, clicks her jaw, and flexes her arm muscles. All these actions are involuntary. Almost five hundred thousand children in the United States live with TS. "I'm very happy to talk about it," Billie said. "So many people have it that you would never know."

Billie, who identifies as queer, first became famous in 2015 when she was fourteen years old. Her song "Ocean Eyes" became a smash sensation. Billie followed up with a full album, *When We All Fall Asleep, Where Do We Go?* At the 2020 Grammy Awards, Billie was the first female and youngest artist (nineteen years old) to win four top awards, including Best New Artist, Record of the Year, Song of the Year, and Album of the Year. In 2021, Billie followed up with another Grammy Award for Best Original Song, "No Time to Die," for the James Bond movie with the same name.

Billie grew up in Los Angeles, California, and was homeschooled by her mother and father. Her parents wanted to give her the time to explore her own passions and interests. It became clear that Billie's passion and talent were singing and songwriting. Her style has been called "whisper singing." She has perfect pitch and uses her breath like an instrument in each of her songs.

In addition to her singing, Billie is an advocate for many causes. She has one hundred and twenty million followers on Instagram and uses this platform to speak about fighting climate change and protecting animal rights. In June 2024, she became the most streamed monthly artist on Spotify. Billie thinks the way we can improve our world and lives—both mentally and physically—is by talking about issues and not pretending challenges and problems don't exist. This is why she is so open about having TS.

"It's not like I like it," Billie explained about living with TS. "But I feel it's part of me. I have made friends with it. And so now, I'm pretty confident in it."

Aretha Franklin

First Woman Inducted into the Rock & Roll Hall of Fame

1942–2018

Aretha Franklin is considered royalty in the music world, and she has the nickname to prove it: the Queen of Soul.

Soul music was born in the 1960s out of the Black experience. It is a combination of gospel, the blues, and pop music. Aretha was one of the first women to sing soul, and when she sang, her voice had such confidence and power that it made people—especially women—feel more confident too.

Aretha grew up in Detroit, Michigan. Her mother was a gospel singer and piano player, and her father was a minister in a Baptist church. Because of her obvious talents, Aretha's father predicted that his young daughter "would sing for kings and queens one day."

When Aretha was in her early teens, she performed in gospel programs all over the country. When she was eighteen, Aretha began singing other types of music besides gospel. She sang everything from Broadway tunes to rhythm and blues.

Aretha recorded her most famous and biggest hit, "Respect" in April 1967 when she was only twenty-five years old. The song and the way Aretha sang it carried an immense emotional punch. "R-E-S-P-E-C-T" became a rallying cry for all people, especially Black people in the fight for civil rights and for women in the fight for equality. The song was a call for social justice reform in the United States, which Aretha cared strongly about. She marched with civil rights leader Dr. Martin Luther King Jr.

"It was the need of the nation, the need of the average man, and woman in the street, the businessman, the mother, the fireman, the teacher—everyone wanted respect," Aretha said about her song.

"Respect" quickly reached number one on the pop charts. Aretha also won her first two Grammy Awards for the song. She went on to record fifty-eight albums, have seventeen top singles, and win eighteen Grammy Awards over the course of her long career. In 1987, she became the first woman to be inducted into the Rock & Roll Hall of Fame.

In 2009, Aretha sang "My Country, 'Tis of Thee" at the first inauguration of the first Black president of the United States, Barack Obama.

"The gift of her music remains to inspire us all," President Obama said about Aretha.

Aretha demanded respect from all of us and for all of us. She will forever be the Queen of Soul.

Joanne Mitsuko Funakoshi

First Asian American Ice Capades Star

BORN 1945

American figure skaters now come from all backgrounds, the only barriers to success being talent and access to top-level coaching. But when Joanne Mitsuko Funakoshi was growing up in the 1950s, there were no Asian American female skaters for her to look up to in the United States. Still, Joanne loved to be on the ice and worked hard to make her dream come true. In 1964, she became the first Asian American skater featured in the world-famous Ice Capades.

Joanne was born in Chicago, but her family moved to Southern California, home of surfing and skateboarding, when she was two years old. Instead of riding the waves, Joanne grew to love ice skating. From the time she was eleven, she was practicing many hours a day. She was only five feet tall but had strength and grace on the ice, spinning, dancing, and trying jumps of different types. She earned trophies and awards, the most prestigious being a silver medal at the 1963 U.S. Figure Skating Championships.

At age nineteen, Joanne attended a tryout for the Ice Capades. Since 1940, the Ice Capades had traveled around the world, demonstrating ice-skating techniques while putting on entertaining music-and-costume-filled performances. After hiring Joanne, George Eby, the president of the troupe said, "I believe Joanne is one of the most exciting young skating stars I have ever seen. She has grace, beauty, and talent."

Joanne debuted with the Ice Capades in Hawaii in June 1964 and skated with them for five years, thrilling audiences around the United States and Canada. Joanne's performance was often the opening act as she danced gracefully across the ice to the sound of classical music. She later moved to another show called *Holiday on Ice* and traveled the world for more than twenty years, delighted every time she laced on her skates to perform.

Since the 1980s and Joanne's achievements, a growing list of Asian American female skaters have achieved world, American, or Olympic championships. This list includes Michelle Kwan, Kristi Yamaguchi, Karen Chen, and Alysa Liu. On the men's side, Nathan Chen became the first Asian American to win gold at the Winter Olympics in 2022.

After retiring from skating in the 1980s, Joanne became a well-known photographer of ice-skating events. The Los Angeles Figure Skating Club also gives out an award named for her to a top artistic skater each year.

Whoopi Goldberg

First Black Woman to Win the EGOT

BORN 1955

For more than forty-five years in the entertainment business, Whoopi Goldberg's varied talents have helped her earn many awards. But four specific trophies made her the first Black woman to earn EGOT status. That rare honor includes people who have an *E*mmy, a *G*rammy, an *O*scar, and a *T*ony—awards for TV, music recording, movies, and Broadway theater.. To be great at so many art forms takes a wide variety of skills, and Whoopi Goldberg has been building those skills her whole life.

She was born Caryn Elaine Johnson in New York City, where she lived with her family in city housing. Young Caryn loved performing, but she didn't love school because she didn't do well in class. Years later, she found out that she had dyslexia, which can make learning to read and write challenging. Still, her family supported her and encouraged her to keep acting.

After doing a few shows in New York, Caryn moved to Los Angeles. She also changed her name to Whoopi Goldberg, making her new first name the name of a fart toy! In LA, she developed a one-woman comedy show about her life. It ended up back in New York on Broadway and was a huge hit.

The one-woman show's success led to Whoopi's first national fame. She played Celie in *The Color Purple* (PG-13) and was nominated for an Academy Award. But it was comedy that led to the first leg of her EGOT in 1986, when she won a Grammy for Best Comedy Album. She added the *O* for *Oscar* in 1990 for Best Supporting Actress in *Ghost* (PG-13). Showing that she had skills offstage as well, Whoopi was a Tony winner in 2002 for her work as a coproducer of the musical *Thoroughly Modern Millie*. After sixteen nominations for Emmys, she wrapped up her EGOT with an Emmy in 2002 for her work on *Beyond Tara: The Extraordinary Life of Hattie McDaniel* (for more on Hattie, see page 68).

Throughout her career, Whoopi has used her fame to speak out on important causes like AIDS research, LGBTQIA+ rights, and antipoverty programs. Among her other honors, she was the first woman given the Mark Twain Prize for American Humor in 2001. Whoopi won a second Emmy in 2009 for her work on *The View*, a daytime talk show. In all, she has earned twenty-five Emmy nominations. Whoopee for Whoopi!

Amanda Gorman

First National Youth Poet Laureate

BORN 1998

Amanda Gorman uses poetry to bring the world together. She hopes her words inspire change for the good in all of us. In 2017, Amanda was named the first ever national youth poet laureate, a position honoring and celebrating top young poets in the United States.

Amanda's most famous poem is titled "The Hill We Climb." Amanda performed this poem at the presidential inauguration of Joseph Biden in January 2021. Less than a month later, she became the first person to recite a poem at a Super Bowl. "The Hill We Climb" is a call for the country to move forward together. Just two weeks earlier, violent protesters had attacked the U.S. Capitol in Washington, DC, to try to stop the peaceful transfer of power from President Donald Trump to President-Elect Biden. When Amanda spoke, the United States was a deeply divided country, so she stood at the podium and passionately called for unity. The *we* instead of an *I* in the title was meant to be meaningful.

"We will not march back to what was," Amanda wrote in the poem, "but move to what shall be." Only twenty-two years old at the time, Amanda was the youngest poet ever to read at a presidential inauguration.

Amanda became very famous after the reading, but she had already been writing and performing poetry for a long time. She grew up in Los Angeles, California, and was raised by a single mother, Joan Wicks, who was an English teacher. She has a twin sister, Gabrielle, and a brother, Spencer. Amanda began writing poetry when she was five years old. As a child, she had trouble saying her *r*'s, so she read poetry out loud to practice words that were hard for her to say.

In 2012, when she was fourteen, Amanda joined WriteGirl, a writing organization that pairs young girls with mentors. Two years later, she became the first youth poet laureate of Los Angeles. In 2016, when Amanda was a senior in high school, she founded her own organization, called One Pen One Page, a writing and leadership program for underserved youths.

Amanda attended Harvard University and graduated in 2020. She is now an activist as much as a poet, speaking out about gun safety, racial equality, and climate change. She published her book of poetry with the title *Call Us What We Carry* in 2021. She intentionally used the word *we* in the title again.

"It's people of color, it's queer people, it's Indigenous people who are saying, 'We belong in the we as much as anybody,'" Amanda explained. "And we are reclaiming not just our time but our shared humanity."

Ashley Graham

First Size 16 Model on the Cover of *Vogue*

BORN 1987

When Ashley appeared on the cover of the February 2017 edition of *Vogue*, she was the first model who wears a size 16—the size of the average American woman—to do so. Usually models on the covers of magazines, in catalogs, and in television commercials are smaller than Ashley, but that is changing thanks to Ashley and her work promoting body positivity.

"I've been confident enough to speak up and show up for the curvy girls of the world," Ashley said, "and I encourage more women to do so as well."

Ashley grew up in Lincoln, Nebraska. When she was just twelve years old, she was discovered by a modeling agency while walking through her local mall. The agent, her friends, and even strangers told Ashley she was "so pretty...for a big girl." She soon signed with the agency and started to travel all over the world doing shoots as a "plus-size" model.

When Ashley graduated high school at age seventeen, she moved to New York City to model full-time. Despite being successful at what she was doing, Ashley struggled with her identity. When she told people she was a model, most looked surprised. These reactions hurt. After years of enduring this pain, Ashley decided to reclaim her body. She started to love herself for being a curvier model and stopped calling herself "plus-size," even when other people did. Because of Ashley, models like her began speaking out against the use of the phrase *plus-size* as well.

"We are calling ourselves what we want to be called," Ashley said. "Women, with shapes that are our own. I believe beauty is beyond size."

Ashley has helped change the way people see and talk about women's bodies in the media. She is proud of her curvy, strong, and powerful physique. She wants women with all different body types to feel the same way. Ashley wants to redefine what it means to be beautiful. She does not allow photos of herself to be retouched, and she uses her social media platforms like TikTok and X to speak out on this issue. She also did a TED talk about body acceptance that went viral. Ashley simply wants all women to love who they are and how they look. "Loving yourself and every size and shape is not a crime; it's a right," she said.

Juanita Hall

First Black Actor to Win a Tony

1901–1968

Broadway is the name of a long street in New York City, but it's also the nickname for the theater district surrounding Times Square. For more than a century, plays and musicals have filled dozens of theaters there. Black actors have been part of shows since the 1920s, though at first mostly in all-Black shows with themes and stories based in Black culture. Those were the first steps in a long journey to Broadway becoming more diverse.

An important milestone in that journey came in 1950, when Juanita Hall became the first Black actor to win a Tony Award, given each year to Broadway's best.

After growing up and learning to sing in New Jersey, Juanita moved across the Hudson River to New York City. She studied at the famous Juilliard School and landed her first role in a Broadway show in 1927 in *Show Boat*, a story set in the American South. *Show Boat* was the first musical with an interracial cast in American theater. While still taking a few onstage roles, by the 1930s, Juanita was leading her own choir in popular shows heard live in theaters and on the radio.

In 1945, World War II ended, and events from that conflict inspired a musical called *South Pacific*. It was set on an island where American soldiers met with Asian and Polynesian people. Juanita's role was as one of the Asian women, a character called Bloody Mary. Juanita's singing and acting lit up the stage, earning praise from critics and fans. At the 1950 Tony Awards, she was named Best Featured Actress, the first Tony ever for a Black actor.

How much did Juanita love performing? During some of the many months she was in *South Pacific*, she was also singing in a nightclub for hours after each night's Broadway performance!

When *South Pacific* was made into a movie, Juanita played Bloody Mary again. She was also in another famous musical called *Flower Drum Song*, written by the same creators as *South Pacific*. Throughout the 1950s, Juanita earned roles in many other musicals, plays, and films. Later in her career, Juanita appeared on TV shows such as *The Ed Sullivan Show* and made jazz and blues records.

The young singer from New Jersey was one of the key people who helped blaze the trail for actors of color on Broadway and around the country.

Larry Hama

First Major Asian American Comic Book Writer

BORN 1949

The pages of comic books and the stories in superhero movies are packed with characters from all around the world and the universe. For many years, however, a small subset of people—white men—were the ones creating these stories. Today, women and people of color are part of making comics of all kinds, and the process of diversifying the world of comic creation is ongoing. One of the pioneers in this field was Larry Hama, who was the first Asian American writer to develop a major line of comic-book heroes.

Larry went to a high school for art and design in New York City, aiming to be a painter. There he met artists with an interest in comics, which he had also drawn when he was a kid. Then when Larry was twenty-one, he was drafted into the U.S. Army and served in Vietnam until 1971.

After his service, Larry spent the 1970s drawing comic books, including some for DC. He joined Marvel Comics full-time in 1980 and was asked to write and create a series based on the line of G.I. Joe toys. This was his biggest job yet—he had to create the stories for more than a dozen characters, craft plots, and write scripts. Though he was the first Asian American who earned such a major role in comics, Larry recalls his race not being a big deal at the time; he said that people didn't have any issues with his background. "If you could draw or write, that's all that counted."

Soon Larry found a way to make an impact for diversity. The only Asian person in the original group of Marvel characters was Storm Shadow. However, Larry "didn't like the fact that the only Asian character was a bad guy." As the person in charge, he decided to change that, and over time, Storm Shadow joined the G.I. Joe side. Also, thanks to Larry's writing, the female G.I. Joe team members got equal billing. Larry said later that female fans positively responded to this. The female characters he wrote are "not treated as any different from the other team members. They're competent, straightforward, and they go ahead and get the job done."

Larry was in charge of *G.I. Joe* comics for more than ten years. He went on to write, draw, or create many other comic characters for comic books, movies, and TV, and he has become a famous figure in the industry for his pioneering and excellent work.

Hamilton Cast

First Musical with a Highly Diverse Cast to Win a Tony

Through 2022, on average, over 66 percent of the actors on New York stages were white. This is why the smash-hit musical *Hamilton* (PG-13 film version) is such an important trailblazer. In 2016, it became the first show with a largely non-white cast to win a Tony Award for Best Musical. The show was nominated for a record sixteen Tony Awards and went on to win eleven of them. The fast-paced rap and hip-hop music won the 2016 Pulitzer Prize for Drama and a Grammy Award for its original cast recording.

Hamilton is the story of American founding father Alexander Hamilton. It is also the story of an immigrant coming to America to try and make a better life for himself. One of the most famous lines of the musical is when Hamilton and another character high-five each other and say in unison, "Immigrants. We get the job done!"

Lin-Manuel Miranda, who is of Puerto Rican descent, wrote the music and lyrics and cast himself in the leading role of Hamilton, even though he is not white. Miranda cast people of color to play most of the historically white characters. American history has often been told through the eyes of powerful white men, and Lin-Manuel wanted to prove that it doesn't have to be this way.

"This is the story of America then, told by America now. It looks like America now," Lin-Manuel said.

When *Hamilton* opened in February 2015, critics and theatergoers alike gave it rave reviews. Lin-Manuel never imagined just how popular the musical would become. Sold-out performances came night after night and year after year. Schoolchildren all over the country memorized every song and lyric. The actors were regular guests on late-night talk shows, and the cast was invited to the White House to perform.

Hamilton opened doors for new musicals with diverse casts to make their debuts as well as older shows to recast parts with actors of color that would have traditionally gone to white performers. The show's success proved theater audiences desire diversity in their performances, and now Broadway is providing them with these opportunities.

"The number one thing I have learned is that people want our stories," said Lin-Manuel. "People actually want stories they haven't heard before. And that only comes when we have a chorus of voices."

Juan Felipe Herrera

First Latino U.S. Poet Laureate

BORN 1948

Since the days of ancient Greece and Rome, the role of the poet was one of public life. In those days, poems were created to mark important events and to honor champions. The tradition began again in England in 1616 when the first poet laureate was named. The United States followed in 1936 with the job of consultant in poetry to the U.S. Congress, which has been called poet laureate since 1986.

Through 2024, more than fifty people have held the post. The first woman was Louise Bogan in 1945. The first Black person was Robert Hayden in 1976. It was not until 2015 that the first Latine U.S. poet laureate was appointed: Juan Felipe Herrera.

Juan's journey to that honor began in the farm fields of California, where his parents worked picking crops. He heard songs and poems from his parent's native Mexico. He also saw them fight for better rights for farm workers. With a love of language from an early age, Juan studied at UCLA and Stanford. He earned a master's degree from the famous writing program at the University of Iowa and went on to teach and write for many years, producing more than thirty books of poetry, fiction, and nonfiction.

In his work, Juan tries to combine his own Mexican American heritage with the ongoing American story. Like the public servant poets of old, he focuses on how poetry can help people. He once said he was "a poet concerned with the plight of people who suffer."

From 2012 to 2015, Juan was the California poet laureate, where he created poems and projects to fight against bullying and encourage people battling cancer. As the U.S. poet laureate, he created a website called La Casa de Colores. People of all ages could contribute their stories of the "house of colors" Juan thought the U. S. should be. He also wrote online articles that highlighted some of the U.S. history found in the Library of Congress. And he began an interactive illustrated story called "The Technicolor Adventures of Catalina Neon" and invited kids around the country to help the story grow.

Writing for young people has always been a part of Juan's work. One of his books, *Portraits of Hispanic Heroes*, for example, includes biographies of twenty people whose stories can inspire the next generation. Juan's term as poet laureate lasted until 2017. He retired from being a professor of poetry but continues to write and create.

James Wong Howe

First Asian American Oscar Winner

1899–1976

Making a movie takes tons of work by a lot of people, but one of the most important jobs is also one of the least known. Most fans are familiar with actors, writers, and directors but have no idea who makes the moving pictures. That's the cinematographer, who oversees the filming process. They are experts in camera technology, light, and more. It's like painting with film. One of the greatest cinematographers ever was James Wong Howe.

Born Wong Tung Jim in China, he moved with his family to Washington State when he was young. There, a teacher changed his name to James Wong Howe, which sadly happened to many students from Asian countries. James relocated to Los Angeles when he was seventeen and found work cleaning the offices of the Famous Players film company. He became interested in the reels of film he swept off the floor and became a camera operator, shooting films of all kinds. He took to the work and quickly became popular with directors and actors.

James was eventually put in charge of all the photography for Famous Players. That meant he not only held, pointed, and focused the cameras; he also decided which lenses to use and how to light each scene. He came up with creative and groundbreaking ways to film, such as perfecting the use of wide-angle lenses. Most cameras were fixed or on wheels; James started using a camera he could hold by himself, creating new senses of movement. For one movie, he wore roller skates while he filmed a boxing match!

During World War II, when America fought against Japan among others, James faced racism from people who thought he was Japanese. Incredibly, it was not until 1943 that a law was passed allowing a small number of people like James and other immigrants from China to become citizens. James was later accused of being a communist after he visited his homeland to work on a movie after the war. And his marriage to French writer Sanora Babb was not legal in California until 1948 due to a law against interracial marriage.

Through it all, James kept doing incredible work. In 1956, after being nominated five earlier times, James earned his first Oscar for Best Cinematography for his work on *The Rose Tattoo*. Seven years later, he won his second Oscar. In all, James was nominated for his work on ten films.

Geri Jewell

First Actor Featured Openly with a Disability on Prime-Time TV

BORN 1956

Geri Jewell was born with cerebral palsy, a disease that caused her to have difficulty controlling the muscles in her body. As a young girl, Geri also had a dream: she would grow up to be an actor. She had never seen anyone like herself on the big screen.

Geri was raised in Orange County, California. Because of her cerebral palsy, Geri talked and walked differently than most other kids. She was picked on and laughed at by classmates because she was different. To cope, Geri decided to use her sense of humor to address her challenges. Instead of classmates laughing at her, she would try and laugh with them.

"I made people laugh," Geri explained. "And it made other people more comfortable. It was a skill I honed from a very early age."

Geri became so good at getting laughs that she decided to become a stand-up comedian. In 1978, when she was twenty-two, Geri began performing at a club in Los Angeles called the Comedy Store. Norman Lear, a famous television producer, saw one of Geri's shows. Norman was a producer for a hit television show called *The Facts of Life*, which was about life at an all-girls boarding school in New York. Norman came up to Geri after her show and said, "You're really funny, kid, but you're way before your time." Geri responded, "So wait a couple months."

Norman went home and wrote a part with Geri in mind. Three months later, he cast Geri as the cousin of a student at *The Facts of Life* school. Appearing in twelve episodes, Geri was the first regularly featured actor with a disability to appear on prime-time television. Playing a character similar to her real-life self and with the same first name, Geri showed millions of viewers that people with cerebral palsy have dreams, have a sense of humor, and live everyday lives just like everybody else.

"After I first appeared, I received thousands of fan letters," Geri said. "I received letters that said, 'You changed my life.'"

Geri's role on *The Facts of Life* also sparked conversations about other disabilities. "I always believed my cerebral palsy was a vehicle to educate and sensitize people," Geri said.

Quincy Jones

First Black Top Executive at a Major American Record Label

BORN 1933

When Quincy Jones was eleven years old, he snuck into a building near an army base. He was hungry and looking for food but found a piano instead. "I tinkered on it for a moment," said Quincy, "and I knew this was it for me, forever."

Quincy attended high school in Seattle, Washington, where he played the trumpet and learned how to arrange music. He traveled across the country to Boston for college but soon left school to go on tour with a band. Quincy encountered a lot of racism while on the road. For example, his band had to have their white bus driver go into restaurants and get food for them because Black people were not allowed to eat at many restaurants.

Quincy continued to tour throughout the 1950s, in the United States and all over Europe. But no matter how much he performed and learned, he did not make a lot of money.

"We had the best jazz band on the planet, and yet we were literally starving," Quincy explained. "That's when I discovered that there was *music*, and there was the *music business*. If I wanted to survive, I would have to learn the difference between the two."

In 1959, Quincy was hired by Mercury Records in New York City as the company's musical director. He arranged a song for popular singer Lesley Gore, called "It's My Party," that went directly to the top of the charts. Two years later, he was promoted to vice president, making him the first Black person to hold a top position at a major American record label.

Quincy composed countless movie scores and produced multiple bestselling albums and songs. He worked with the biggest stars in history, from Ray Charles to Frank Sinatra.

In 1981, Quincy produced and arranged the record *Thriller* for Michael Jackson. *Thriller* became the bestselling album of all time. Four years later, Quincy gathered forty-six of the most famous musicians in the world—most of whom he had already worked with—to record the single "We Are the World" to raise money to stop world hunger. The song became the biggest-selling single ever, raising over fifty-five million dollars.

In 2013, Quincy was inducted into the Rock & Roll Hall of Fame when he was eighty years old. For most of his career, Quincy can look at the landscape of popular music, which he directly shaped, and say proudly, "It's my party."

Mindy Kaling

First South Asian American Writer and Star of a Major TV Show

BORN 1979

Breaking barriers takes timing and talent...and courage. With skills that include writing, acting, producing, directing, and more, Mindy Kaling has been knocking down barriers since she began her busy career. In 2012, Mindy's talent and tenacity made her the first South Asian American writer and star of a major TV show.

She was born Vera Mindy Chokalingam in Massachusetts, the daughter of parents who had moved to the United States from India. (She uses her middle name and part of her last name as her stage name.) Mindy went to Dartmouth College, where she found a home with the school's comedy troupe and as a writer for the humor magazine. An early career break was her summer internship on the Conan O'Brien TV talk show.

Mindy moved to New York after college to pursue a writing career, and a play she wrote with a Dartmouth classmate, called *Matt & Ben*, was a comedy hit. Her writing and acting on that project helped her win a job as a writer—the only female writer—on *The Office* (TV-14), the American version of a British TV hit. Showing another of her many talents, Mindy soon began appearing in front of the camera while later taking on jobs as a director and producer. Mindy and the writing staff were nominated for numerous Emmy Awards.

Mindy's work as a creative force on *The Office* led to Fox Studios striking a deal with her to create her own show. The result was *The Mindy Project* (TV-14), which debuted in 2012 with Mindy as the creator, writer, and star, making her the first American actor with a South Asian background to hold all those jobs for a major network television show. Mindy played a doctor, and the show followed her life and friends in New York City. It ran for six seasons on Fox and Hulu before ending in 2017.

After *The Mindy Project* concluded, Mindy created a popular show for Netflix called *Never Have I Ever* (TV-14) that featured numerous South Asian American actors and a diverse cast. Her success has given her the power to help change how such shows are made. "For all of us in the writers' room, particularly those of us who were the children of immigrants, which comprised most of my staff, it was about sharing those stories of feeling 'other,'" she said.

Mindy continues to be a creative force in Hollywood, working as a screenwriter, actor, producer, and more. In 2022, she also launched her own book publishing imprint, Mindy's Book Studio, for underrepresented authors, while raising three children.

Alexandra Kutas

First Runway Model in a Wheelchair

BORN 1993

Alexandra Kutas believes beauty is revealed in different ways. "Your gender, [the] color of your skin, your mental or physical challenges, should not define who you are and what you are capable of doing," Alexandra said.

Alexandra is the first model in a wheelchair to be featured on the runway. A runway model is a person who appears in fashion shows wearing fabulous designer clothes while posing for photographers. Most models walk down the runway. That is until Alexandra came on the scene.

Alexandra grew up in Dnipro, Ukraine. When she was born, she suffered a spinal cord injury that left her paralyzed from the waist down. In 2009, when Alexandra was sixteen, she was eating lunch in a café when a photographer spotted her. The photographer thought Alexandra was beautiful and asked if she could take her picture. That encounter launched Alexandra's career and mission. "I loved the process of creating images," Alexandra explained. "I felt more alive."

Alexandra began sending photographs of herself to modeling agencies in America and all over the world. Many of the agencies responded and said she was pretty, but the modeling world was not ready for a model in a wheelchair. She studied psychology at a university in Ukraine, and her interest in becoming a fashion model continued to grow. In 2015 when she was twenty-two, she created a series of photographs of herself sitting in her wheelchair wrapped in chains. Alexandra launched this exhibit to show people how to break free of their own prejudices. She did many interviews about the exhibit and used social media to spread the word about the message behind her photographs.

Thanks to the positive response, Alexandra made her debut as the first runway model in a wheelchair at a 2015 fashion show in Ukraine. She was stunningly dressed in a long black ball gown. In 2016, she took the United States by storm when she modeled at New York Fashion Week—one of the most famous fashion weeks in the world.

In addition to working as a model, Alexandra is also a disability activist. She works to make city streets and businesses more accessible in her home city of Dnipro. Additionally, Alexandra started her own fashion line, Puffins Fashion, which makes stylish clothes for people with disabilities.

"Unfortunately, diversity in the fashion world is still quite fragmented," she said. "I'm the world's first runway model in a wheelchair, but I want to make sure I won't be the last one."

Edmonia Lewis

First Successful Black Indigenous American Sculptor

1844–1907

Edmonia Lewis had just about everything working against her as she forged a career as a sculptor. In the late 1800s, women were rarely recognized in the field. She was also Black and Chippewa, which forced her to leave the United States for Europe to pursue her art without facing slavery and, later on, racist laws and attitudes. But she overcame all those challenges to emerge as the first person of color to make a lasting mark in American sculpture.

Edmonia was born near Albany, New York. Her father was a Black man from Haiti; her mother was of the Chippewa nation. Some reports say her mother gave her the tribal name of Wildfire. Sadly, both her parents died when Edmonia was young, and she was raised by two aunts. Another relative made money in the California gold rush and was able to pay for her to study at Oberlin College in Ohio, one of the few schools in the country in the late 1850s that accepted Black women.

Unfortunately, her time there was hard, as she was accused of poisoning classmates. She was even attacked and beaten in revenge at one point. The charges against her were all dropped, but she left school and moved to Boston. There she connected with important abolitionists (people who fought against slavery), who supported her as she continued to study. At first, Edmonia sold ceramic medallions showing famous faces. But the American art scene did not accept her as a Black Indigenous woman, so she moved to the more accepting Europe, ending up in Rome.

As she began selling her art in Rome, she became quite well-known, and famous artists and others visited her studio. Still, she was frustrated that she had to leave America to achieve her success. "I was practically driven to Rome...to find a social atmosphere where I was not constantly reminded of my color," she said in 1878.

Her greatest sculpture was *The Death of Cleopatra*, which took her four years to make. It was exhibited at a major show in Philadelphia. After going through many hands after her death, the work now holds a special place at the Smithsonian American Art Museum.

Today, Edmonia's work is found in several U.S. museums, including the Metropolitan Museum of Art in New York City, and art museums in Detroit, Baltimore, and Washington, DC, among other places. An artist who might have been headed to invisibility instead wound up in places of honor.

Jennifer Lopez

First Latina to Earn Over a Million Dollars for a Film

BORN 1969

Jennifer Lopez wasn't always the famous triple threat—actor, singer, and dancer—that she is now. In fact, she was relatively unknown in 1997 when she was cast to play Selena Quintanilla (page 90) in the movie *Selena*. Playing Selena, Jennifer became the first Latina actor to earn over a million dollars from one film. This also opened a space for other Latina performers to follow in her path. "When I went into these worlds like Hollywood, where we were not represented at all, I almost felt like a unicorn," Jennifer said about her barrier-breaking role.

Jennifer was raised in the Bronx, New York. Her parents were both born in Puerto Rico but moved to the United States during her childhood. Jennifer's parents taught their daughter to be proud of her Latin heritage and culture. Jennifer's mother loved musicals, and her enthusiasm made Jennifer love them too. "I always thought the singing, dancing, acting combination was something I would want to do," Jennifer said.

In 1990, Jennifer began her professional career as a dancer on a television comedy show called *In Living Color* (TV-14). When she landed the lead role of Selena seven years later at age twenty-eight, her career skyrocketed. "When I was a young actor, good roles for women of color were very limited," Jennifer explained. "But I just kept grinding and believing that someday I would get that shot."

In 2001, she became the first woman to have a number one album (*J.Lo*) and a number one movie (*The Wedding Planner*, PG-13) in the same week. She was a judge on the singing competition show *American Idol* from 2011 to 2018. As of 2023, Jennifer has sold over eighty million records and made more than forty movies that have grossed above three billion dollars. She also has her own fashion and perfume line.

As Jennifer's career flourishes, she has made it a point to help the Latine community right along with her. She launched Limitless Labs, which helps finance Latine-owned small businesses as well as offer mentorship opportunities for Latina women who live in underserved communities.

"I want to empower every woman to create the most beautiful life that they [can] for themselves," Jennifer said.

Matthew López

First Latino to Win a Tony for Best Play

BORN 1977

Matthew López's play *The Inheritance* made its debut on Broadway in November 2019. Soon after, it won many awards, including the Tony Award for Best Play, making Matthew the first Latino writer ever to win the honor. This was *73 years* after the Tony Awards were founded.

In Matthew's acceptance speech, he encouraged the theater industry to give other Latine artists opportunities to write too. "We are a vibrant community reflecting a vast array of cultures, experiences, and, yes, skin tones," Matthew said. "We have so many stories to tell. They are inside of us aching to come out. Let us tell you our stories."

Matthew grew up in Panama City, Florida. From an early age, Matthew knew he was gay and felt isolated from friends and classmates because of this. He also felt alone because he was one of only a few Latine people in his community. He wrestled with feeling different from others his whole childhood. "There was nobody like [my family] around," Matthew said. "I went through a very shameful period where I didn't like my last name."

Matthew went to college at the University of Southern Florida and studied theater performance. He then moved to New York City to become an actor in January 2000 when he was twenty-two years old. Instead of acting though, he picked up a notebook and began writing. Matthew's first breakout play came six years later. It was set right after the Civil War and was about two freed slaves and the man who had enslaved them. The play was loved by adult audiences and critics alike.

Matthew wrote his most personal play, *Somewhere*, soon after. *Somewhere* made its debut in 2011 and featured an almost entirely Latine cast. It is set in New York City in the 1950s around a theatrical family who is fighting to save their neighborhood.

When Matthew isn't writing, he works to make the theater world a more inclusive place for all—especially for his Latine community.

"When I was growing up, there were very few examples for me to look to," Matthew said. "I now have the opportunity to open that door for others."

ANTOINETTE PERRY AWARD
AMERICAN THEATRE WING

Marlee Matlin

First Deaf Person to Win an Oscar

BORN 1965

When Marlee Matlin first saw actor and costar William Hurt announce her name in sign language from the stage at the 1987 Academy Awards, she thought he was teasing her. William was not. Instead, he was telling Marlee she had won the Oscar for Best Actress in a Leading Role in their film, *Children of a Lesser God* (R). She was the first deaf actor to win this award, and at twenty-one years and two hundred and eighteen days old, she was the youngest actor to ever win as well.

Once the crowd stopped applauding, silence swept across the venue. Marlee used American Sign Language to give her acceptance speech, showing the millions of viewers how many deaf people communicate, while her interpreter put voice to her words. Marlee ended her speech with two simple signs: "Thank you" and "I love you."

Marlee grew up outside Chicago, Illinois, with two older brothers. She got sick with a virus when she was eighteen months old and lost her hearing. Marlee was the only deaf person in her household; sometimes this was very hard and isolating.

"Anyone else in the family could pick up the phone and call my grandmother," Marlee wrote in her autobiography. "I wanted to, but I couldn't."

Marlee found her community when she began acting at age eight at the International Center on Deafness and the Arts near her home. The center put on plays and musicals that included both hearing and deaf children, and Marlee's first role was as Dorothy in *The Wizard of Oz*. She has been acting ever since, working in film and TV for over thirty years.

In addition to her Oscar, she won a Golden Globe and has been nominated for four Emmy Awards. In 2021, Marlee was also a costar in the movie *CODA* (PG-13), which became the first movie to win the Academy Award for Best Picture with a mostly deaf cast. In August 2024, PBS created a documentary about Matlin and used ASL as the primary language.

Marlee is a strong advocate for the deaf community. She fought for films and television shows to include closed captions, which is when the words that the actors speak are written across the screen. She wants to make sure closed captioning is an option not just in the United States but for programming in countries all over the world—including Australia, England, France, and Italy. She also created an app, Marlee Signs, that helps people learn sign language in developing countries.

"It's up to all of us who have succeeded in overcoming barriers to use any means to communicate that we all deserve to stand equally with one another," Marlee said.

Darryl McCray (Cornbread)

World's First Modern Graffiti Artist

BORN 1953

While graffiti has long been controversial, it has existed as an art form since ancient Rome. Graffiti is when words or drawings are written on public walls and buildings. The people who do graffiti, called *graffiti artists*, use spray paint to scrawl words or make bold, beautiful drawings. Sometimes the artists are hired by the city to make graffiti drawings. Other times, they do it illegally without being asked. Darryl McCray—otherwise known as Cornbread—is a trailblazer in this field.

Cornbread is the world's first famous graffiti artist. He first became known in the late 1960s and early 1970s by spray-painting his nickname, Cornbread, all over the city of Philadelphia, Pennsylvania. Darryl was born and raised in this city. His neighborhood had gangs, and there was a lot of fighting and violence that happened as a result.

"I didn't deal with what was going on in the streets—the gang wars, the fighting," said Cornbread. "I was spray-painting."

When Cornbread was twelve years old, he was sent to a youth development facility, where he got his nickname. While there, he asked the cook in the kitchen to make cornbread for dinner (he loved cornbread). Cornbread asked the cook for this dinner so much, the cook gave him his nickname.

Once Cornbread was out of the center at age fourteen, he began writing his name, called *tagging*, with spray paint all over the city. At first, it was more about frequency than it was about making art. He wanted to make a name for himself, and he did it by writing his name everywhere.

Cornbread has been creating graffiti now for over fifty years. His work has appeared in art galleries in Philadelphia and in Brooklyn, New York. He was inducted into the Graffiti Hall of Fame in New York City in 2013.

These days, Cornbread helps out with the Mural Arts Program in Philadelphia. The program creates murals—large paintings on walls in public places—all over the city that inspire and promote pride. They are also a way to create a more unified art space. More than one hundred murals are created every year.

"At the end of the day, I'd like to be recognized fully for the culture that I gave birth to," he said. "There was no graffiti artist before me. All roads lead back to me."

CORNBREAD

Hattie McDaniel

First Black Actor to Win an Oscar

1893–1952

In early 1940, the famous movie *Gone with the Wind* was up for several Oscars, including Hattie McDaniel for Best Supporting Actress. But since the Academy Awards took place at a segregated Los Angeles hotel, Hattie could not even sit at the same table as her fellow actors because she was Black.

Hattie's road to Hollywood fame began in Kansas as the youngest of thirteen children. Her family later moved to Denver, where Hattie began singing and performing. By the 1920s, she had appeared in theaters and on radio shows. She moved to Los Angeles in 1931; three of her older siblings had gone there earlier. While trying to kick-start her film career, Hattie worked as a maid in houses. Later, almost all her movie roles were as maids because that was one of the few roles that Black women were allowed to play in racist Hollywood.

In *Gone with the Wind*, Hattie played the part of an enslaved woman known only as Mammy, a stereotypical term for a black maid. It was a controversial movie since it showed slavery in a positive light during the Civil War. Black leaders were upset and asked that changes be made to the film, but few were. Some black viewers were also upset that Hattie had accepted such a stereotyped role. For her part, Hattie once said "I can be a maid for seven dollars a week. Or I can *play* a maid for seven hundred dollars a week." Still, roles like Mammy are often seen as a backward step for diversity in movies.

Gone with the Wind was set around Atlanta, and the producers held the movie's premiere there. Hattie and other Black actors were not allowed to attend. The film's star, Clark Gable, and others threatened not to attend in protest, but Hattie told them to go ahead. The film earned many Oscar nominations, including one for Hattie, the first for a Black actor. So, when Hattie won for Best Supporting Actress, she was the first Black actor—male or female—to win an Oscar. After Hattie, no other Black female actor won until Whoopi Goldberg (page 32) in 1992.

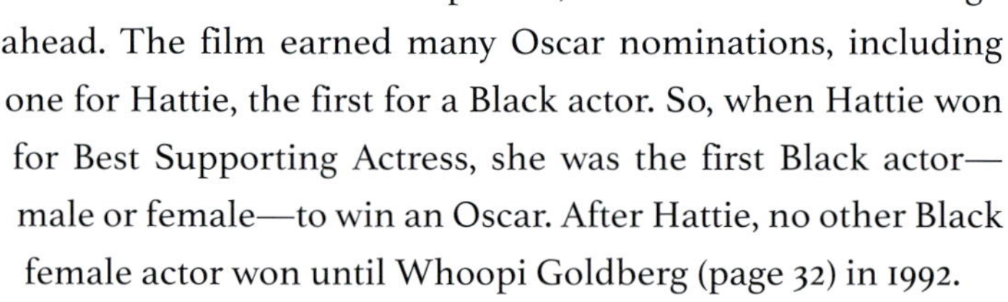

Hattie went on to make many other movies, and in 1947, she became the first Black female actor to headline a national radio program, *The Beulah Show*. In 2006, the U.S. Postal Service put Hattie on a stamp, honoring her pioneering presence in movies and entertainment.

Oscar Micheaux

First Well-Known Black Filmmaker

1884–1951

Using lessons he learned by doing everything himself on a South Dakota farm, Oscar Micheaux was a one-person creative force. He wrote, directed, filmed, and produced more than forty movies as the first major Black filmmaker in American history.

Oscar was born in Illinois in 1884 and moved to South Dakota late in his teens. After working at several jobs, he became a railroad porter, one of the few good-paying jobs open to Black men at the time. In 1906, he bought a plot of land in South Dakota. Farming work was hard, and he later had to sell his land, but his experiences inspired him to write a novel based on his life. It was published in 1912, and Oscar even went door-to-door to sell it!

In 1919, he turned his novel into a movie, *The Homesteader*. It was the first feature-length movie created by a Black person in the U.S. Like he did on the farm, Oscar did it all: wrote, filmed, directed, and produced. As he made more movies, Oscar gave work to Black actors and other creative people while at the same time trying to tell audiences about the Black experience. In *Within Our Gates*, for example, Oscar filmed a story that warned of the dangers and evils of white supremacy. Importantly, in Oscar's films—and those by other Black creators—Black actors could take on roles that white Hollywood films did not allow, such as private eyes, bankers, or elected officials.

Most of Oscar's films were shown at theaters for only Black audiences, but a few broke through into mainstream white movie palaces. Oscar also showed his films in Europe and South America. In 1931, Oscar made a movie that had sound, the first by a Black filmmaker. He also inspired others to follow, and by the 1930s, dozens of Black moviemakers were creating what were known at the time as "race films." Like Oscar's movies, they were aimed mostly at Black audiences and featured Black actors and writers.

As a filmmaker, Oscar's greatness lies in the fact that he persisted through various limitations, learning and growing as he went. He made a career in film at a time when very few Black people were part of the movie industry. Most importantly, Black filmmakers of today point to Oscar's pioneering work as an inspiration.

Coco Mitchell

Pioneering Black Model

BIRTHDATE UNKNOWN

Coco was a model in the early stages of her career when she was sent on a casting call, which is like an interview for a modeling job. When Coco arrived, the designer said to her, "Who sent you here?" When Coco answered that she was sent by her agent, the racist designer responded, "I told your agency we didn't want any Black girls."

"They didn't book me," Coco acknowledged. "But I did handle myself."

Coco has had to battle racism over the course of her career, but it hasn't stopped her from being one of the most successful models on the runway. In 1986, when Coco was in her thirties, she was one of the first Black models to appear in the *Sports Illustrated* swimsuit issue. Now in her sixties, Coco is still walking the runway and is a sought-after model for many clothing companies. She also works tirelessly to make sure what happened to her doesn't happen to other Black models who have followed.

"I have always been in the fight for diversity," Coco said. "No matter how many times you tell me no, I am going to keep coming back. There are other people behind me who have to have a chance."

Coco grew up in Florida and went to college to become an elementary teacher. After graduation in 1977, she moved to New York City for a teaching job. She was walking home from her school in Manhattan one day when Eileen Ford, a famous modeling executive, noticed Coco's striking looks and asked her to try modeling. Coco gave up teaching by the end of the school year and began modeling full-time. She traveled all over the world, modeling in shows as well as in magazines and advertisements. In the late 1970s, Coco was part of the beauty company Revlon's first Black-women-centered campaign.

Coco is admired for her inclusion work in the modeling world as well as her longevity as a model. She has modeled for over fifty years.

"I'll work until they stop booking me," she said in one interview. "I'm here to help people understand that me being the only Black person in the room is not an honor. It's an insult."

Coco continues to work to get more Black models like her as many opportunities as possible. Designers continually consult Coco as their diversity expert, and she is happy to be such a voice.

Rita Moreno

First Latina to Win the EGOT

BORN 1931

Rita Moreno has so many talents, it took four awards to honor her achievements. After becoming the first Latina to win an Oscar in 1961, she added an Emmy, Grammy, and Tony. That made her the first Latine person—and one of only nineteen men or women through early 2024—to achieve legendary EGOT status. It's hard to say what Moreno is more famous for: her all-around entertainment talents or her pioneering work for women and Hispanic performers.

Rita was born Rosa Dolores Alverío Marcano in Puerto Rico. When she was six, she moved with her family to New York City, where she took lessons in Spanish dancing and singing, later taking part in shows in clubs. When she was thirteen, she earned her first role in a Broadway show.

After signing a contract with MGM to act in movies, she took on her stage name. Rita came from a top Hollywood star, Rita Hayworth. Moreno was her stepfather's last name. She earned small movie roles in the 1950s, often cast in stereotyped roles as women of different ethnic backgrounds. Her big break came when she played Anita in the film of a successful Broadway show, *West Side Story*. The musical retelling of Romeo and Juliet told the story of racial clashes between white and Puerto Rican teenagers in New York City, and Rita had several solo singing and dancing moments. Her enthusiastic performance made her the first Latina to win an Oscar, for Best Supporting Actress.

In the 1960s, Rita acted mostly in theater, as the roles offered by movies continued to be stereotypes. In 1963, she took part in the March for Jobs and Freedom with other actors in support of Dr. Martin Luther King Jr. In 1972, she got her next EGOT award, a Grammy for her work on an album of songs from *The Electric Company*, a kids' TV show she was on. Three years later, she earned her Tony for Best Featured Actress in a play called *The Ritz*. In 1977, she became just the third person—and first Latine person—to earn the coveted EGOT, thanks to an acting Emmy for *The Electric Company*.

Rita has continued to take on leading roles on TV, on the stage, and in movies while working to inspire other young Latine actors, and in 2009, President Barack Obama honored her with the prestigious National Medal of Arts.

Toni Morrison

First Black Woman to Win a Nobel Prize in Literature

1931–2019

When author Toni Morrison was in her fifties, she sat on her porch at her New York home and enjoyed the view of the Hudson River. Suddenly, an idea for her next book struck her like a bolt of lightning. "It was all like a flood when I wrote that book," Toni said.

When Toni's idea was put down on paper, it became the novel *Beloved*. In 1988, Toni won the Pulitzer Prize for Fiction for *Beloved*. Six years later in 1994, she became the first Black woman to win the Nobel Prize in Literature for her overall body of work. The Nobel Prize is the most outstanding award a writer can receive.

"Winning the [Nobel] prize was fabulous," Toni said. "I felt American. I felt Blacker than ever. I felt more woman than ever. I felt all of that."

The story of *Beloved* was inspired by a real-life story of a woman who escaped slavery. Like much of Toni's writing, the plot focused on the lives of Black people and the consequences of racism, enslavement, abuse, and poverty in America. Toni gave voice to people of color—especially Black women—and their experiences. She did it in an intentional and complex way.

Toni was born Chloe Anthony Wofford in Lorain, Ohio. She grew up in a working-class neighborhood. Her father was a ship welder, and her mother cooked and cleaned in other people's homes. Toni always loved to read. She also enjoyed listening to her grandmother tell stories about life down in the South. Her grandmother loved to tell ghost stories. All these tales influenced Toni's future works.

Toni wrote eleven novels over the course of her almost sixty-year career. Her novels have been translated into more than twenty different languages. She also wrote many essays and children's books. In 2012, when Toni was eighty-one, she was awarded the Presidential Medal of Freedom, which is the highest award a civilian can win. Toni's novels can be heartbreaking to read because they focus on themes that include violence and the shameful and persistent consequences of slavery. But what Toni wrote was true—true to her heart and true to the past. She knew this was her most important job as a writer.

"I am a storyteller and therefore an optimist," she said. "[I am] a believer in the mind's appetite for truth and its disgust with fraud."

Viet Thanh Nguyen

First Asian American to Win Pulitzer Prize for Fiction

BORN 1971

Joseph Pulitzer emigrated from Hungary to the United States and became a newspaper editor in the late 1800s. His will created the Pulitzer Prize, given to writers in different fields, including fiction. The prize was almost a century old, however, before an Asian American earned the fiction prize—Viet Thanh Nguyen for his 2015 novel *The Sympathizer*. Incredibly, it was Viet's first book!

Like Pulitzer, Viet arrived in America as an immigrant, coming with his family to Pennsylvania in 1975. His family later moved to San Jose, California, where his parents opened a small grocery store. As they struggled to rebuild their lives in their new home, they encouraged Viet to follow his dreams.

Those dreams took him to the University of California, Berkeley, where he studied literature and writing. While he was there, a professor told him *not* to write a research paper on Vietnamese American books. The professor meant that there was so little interest in that topic, Viet would not be able to find a job teaching it after he graduated! Viet persisted and earned a doctorate in English. He also began a lifelong focus on speaking out against injustice. "I was always outspoken," he said. "The book just gave me a bigger platform to say everything I was always saying."

The Sympathizer was published in 2015 and was an immediate hit. An adult spy novel, it was also a deep look at how the Vietnam War affected people in Vietnam, the United States, and France, a former colonizer of Vietnam. Viet was both surprised and honored when it was announced that his book had won the Pulitzer Prize. The book won many other prizes, too, including from the Mystery Writers of America and the Asian/Pacific American Literature Award.

Now a professor at the University of Southern California, Viet earned another first in 2020 as the first Asian American named to the board that selects Pulitzer winners. In 2021, he published a sequel to *The Sympathizer* called *The Committed*. He also wrote a nonfiction book about the Vietnam War called *Nothing Ever Dies: Vietnam and the Memory of War*, and a children's book called *Chicken of the Sea*. For that title, he got help from his young son, Elliott!

Sierra Teller Ornelas

First Indigenous American TV Showrunner

BORN 1981

Being creative runs in the family of Sierra Teller Ornelas. For more than six generations, her family members have created Navajo weavings, but Sierra found her own outlet for creativity and became the first Indigenous American to create and run her own TV show.

Sierra was born in Tucson, Arizona. Her family is part of the Edge Water clan of the Navajo Nation. Before Sierra got to high school, she saw the power of creativity to change lives. Her family worked together to create a large piece of weaving art, which they sold for a lot of money. The weaving changed their lives, giving them all new opportunities.

At the University of Arizona, Sierra found her own avenue for creativity, discovering a love of comedy, writing, and performing. After spending a few years after college working at the Smithsonian Museum of the American Indian in Washington, DC, she made the move to Los Angeles to try her hand at writing for TV. She got jobs writing for shows like *Superstore* (TV-14) and *Brooklyn Nine-Nine* (TV-14).

In 2021, she was brought onto the team developing a new show called *Rutherford Falls* (TV-14). Because the show was set in a Native American nation, she was the perfect person to become the showrunner, a TV term for the person in charge of all aspects of production. She was also the first Indigenous person to hold such a job. At meetings to sell the comedy, which is about the culture clash between a white historian and Indigenous Americans, Sierra made sure to show off her Navajo-style jewelry and silver.

"It has been a long time coming," she said. "We were the first storytellers. But the system dictated that we weren't able to tell these stories from our own perspective." In fact, Sierra's family name, given to her great-great-grandfather by American soldiers in the late 1800s, comes from his tribal role as an actual storyteller. For Sierra, "working in television is just the continuation of his art form." Sierra also made sure that Indigenous people took part as actors, directors, and creators of costumes and music. She was especially pleased with the custom beadwork artists made for the show's characters.

Unfortunately, *Rutherford Falls* only lasted two seasons, though Sierra said they hope to find a new studio to produce it. In any case, she said, it was "a breakthrough moment for Native American representation." She continues to write and create TV shows.

Megan Piphus Peace

First Black Woman to be a Puppeteer on *Sesame Street*

BORN 1992

The kids TV show *Sesame Street* is so well-known for its inclusion and diversity, Megan Piphus Peace was shocked to learn that she was its first Black female puppeteer. (Kevin Clash, a Black male puppeteer, worked on *Sesame Street* in the 1980s, performing as Elmo and other characters, but no Black woman ever had.) Still, given Megan's lifelong love of the show and her talents as a performer, she knew she had found her home on that familiar TV street.

Megan was born in Cincinnati and was a *Sesame Street* fan early on. Her love of the show inspired her to learn puppetry. She also taught herself ventriloquism, which is the skill of speaking in different voices but with your mouth closed. (Try talking without moving your lips. It's harder than it looks!) By the time she was a teenager, Megan's skills had taken her to national TV appearances including *The Tonight Show* and Oprah Winfrey's talk show. She even gave her high school graduation speech as a ventriloquist, using a puppet named George.

Knowing that there are very few jobs as a full-time puppeteer, Megan studied finance at Vanderbilt University. She kept performing, however, as the Vanderbilt Ventriloquist. She won a local Emmy Award for helping make a TV show with puppets that taught kids about money and finance. After graduating, she worked in real estate while continuing to perform, including appearing on shows in Italy and Germany.

In 2020, Megan auditioned for a spot in the *Sesame Street* troupe of puppeteers. While auditioning, she helped make a *Sesame Street* special for CNN. The show's producers saw how skilled she was, and in 2021, she was hired full-time. She is the voice of the character Gabrielle, who is a six-year-old Black girl. "I want her confidence to just shine through the screen so that little girls and boys around the world are filled with confidence in themselves," said Megan about her puppet.

The award-winning show has included lessons and stories about race and equality from its beginnings in the 1960s, with both puppets and live actors from many backgrounds. But Megan was thrilled with her specific groundbreaking efforts. "I'm so glad [to have] the opportunity to be on *Sesame Street* and encourage other kids to dream as big as their imaginations will allow," she said.

Jerry Pinkney

First Black Solo Illustrator to Win the Caldecott Medal

1939–2021

Children's book illustrator Jerry Pinkney drew what he knew and what he wanted others—especially children—to know. Pinkney's drawings depicted Black characters and Black history, experience, and lifestyle. This was rare in the children's book business—especially when Jerry started in 1964—where almost all the children in books were drawn as white. Additionally, most of the illustrators and writers in the business were white as well.

"I wanted to show that an African American artist could make it in this country on a national level in the graphic arts," Jerry said. "I wanted to be a strong role model for my family and for other African Americans."

In 2010, when Jerry was seventy-one years old, he became the first Black solo illustrator to win the Caldecott Medal for his book *The Lion and the Mouse*. The Caldecott is awarded for the best American illustrated children's book. Pinkney's book was a retelling of Aesop's fable with the same name. Even in a book about a lion and a mouse, Pinkney made sure that African themes were present: The almost wordless book was set in the Serengeti, a preserved wildlife area in Tanzania. The animal characters in the book were surrounded by Tanzanian wildlife throughout the pages.

Jerry was born and grew up in Philadelphia, Pennsylvania. He struggled to learn to read as a child, but he was always good at drawing. Jerry and his family were not always welcome in the same stores and public places as white people. Jerry used his drawing to escape this reality.

"I was able to be anything and go anywhere," Jerry said about his drawing.

Jerry attended college at the Philadelphia Museum College of Art and worked briefly as an illustrator at a greeting card company. He illustrated his first book in 1964 and soon started illustrating full-time. He worked on over one hundred books over almost a sixty-year career. Five of his books were named Caldecott Honor Books. He also won five Coretta Scott King Awards from the American Library Association and won a Lifetime Achievement Award from the Society of Illustrators in 2006. He was inducted into their Hall of Fame in 2011.

"I am a storyteller at heart," Jerry said about his body of work. "There is something special about knowing that your stories can alter the way people see the world and their place within it."

Billy Porter

First Openly Gay Black Man to Win an Emmy for Lead Actor

BORN 1969

Billy Porter is a fashion icon. This means he is admired for the stylish clothes he wears. But Billy doesn't just push fashion boundaries—he flies over them. He wears bright colors, giant headpieces, and gender-fluid outfits. And Billy doesn't think the way he dresses is a big deal.

"People say, 'I could never pull that off,'" Billy explains. "You know how you pull it off? Put it on."

Billy isn't just fashion-forward; he is forward-thinking in every aspect of his life. In 2019, Billy became the first openly gay Black man to win an Emmy Award for a lead acting role in the show *Pose* (TV-MA).

"I am just so grateful that I've lived long enough to see the day where I could stand up in front of the world as my true authentic self," Billy said.

Billy's journey to arrive as an Emmy Award-winning actor was a rocky one. He grew up in Pittsburgh, Pennsylvania, with a single mother who remarried when Billy was seven. Billy knew he was gay from a young age, and his classmates beat him up because of this.

"My Black queerness made everyone uncomfortable," he said.

Billy's life changed for the better once he discovered musical theater. He performed in high school and then in college at Carnegie Mellon University in Pittsburgh.

During his senior year, Billy earned an ensemble part in the musical *Miss Saigon* on Broadway in New York City. After graduating college in 1991, Billy moved to New York for good. He landed small parts in musicals and on television shows for years before being cast as Lola in the musical *Kinky Boots*. For this starring role, he won the 2013 Tony Award for Lead Actor in a Musical. Years later, he played the Fabulous Godmother in an Amazon adaptation of *Cinderella*.

Billy is proud of all his accomplishments and of course his sense of style. But he is most proud of pushing the conversation forward about the importance of diversity in every walk of life. "We're ready for a new story to be told," Billy said, and he is part of telling that story.

Richard Potter

First Black American Professional Magician

1783–1835

Talented performers cannot make racism disappear—not even Richard Potter, the first Black magician in the United States. Still, Richard bravely broke down many racial barriers and was so well-known in his time that some historians call him the first Black celebrity in U.S. history.

Richard was born in Massachusetts. His mother had been an enslaved person but was later freed, and his father was a white man about whom little is known. When Richard was a teenager, he learned some magic tricks and tightrope walking during a short visit to Europe. When he returned, he met a Scottish magician named James Rannie and traveled with him as an assistant. From Rannie, Richard learned many of the skills that would make his fortune. One was the ability to "throw" his voice, a type of ventriloquism done without the traditional puppet.

Richard took over the act after Rannie retired. By 1811, Richard was drawing big crowds to theaters in Boston and other northeast cities at a time when few Black performers were even allowed in white venues. Along with ventriloquism, where he made teapots "talk," he created the illusion of an invisible bird flying in the theater. Richard also performed magic tricks like a disappearing egg, vanishing and reappearing coins, and an odd routine that involved a headless chicken. Richard would later add singing, dancing, and acting to his performances, sometimes including his wife onstage.

Throughout his long performing career, Richard never hid the fact that he was Black, but he also didn't advertise it. He just amazed audiences with his talent. By 1814, Richard was so successful that he bought land in New Hampshire and built a grand house. A historic marker nearby notes that the former railroad depot there was called Potter Place. Though he made a lot of money as a magician, Richard's travels were not always simple. When he toured the South in 1820, he was refused service at some hotels and threatened by thieves at another stop. Even so, said biographer John Hodgson, "Richard Potter was the most famous Black man in America in the 1820s and 1830s."

Richard's life story almost vanished like one of the coins in his act, but famous magician Harry Houdini wrote about Richard in the 1930s, cementing his legacy. Hodgson's 2018 biography of Richard has also helped spread the word about this unique entertainment pioneer.

POTTER
NO KNOWN IMAGES OF RICHARD POTTER EXIST

Selena Quintanilla

First Latina Solo Artist to Debut at #1 on the Billboard 200

1971–1995

You know you are one of the world's biggest stars if everybody knows you by your first name. This was Selena. Selena was one of the most famous Mexican American singers ever. She rose to fame belting out Tejano music. This is a type of Latin music that combines jazz, country, and polka and includes accordion and guitar accompaniment. The word *Tejano* also means a Mexican American who lives in southern Texas.

Selena Quintanilla was born and raised in a Mexican American family in Texas, close to the Mexican border. She embraced both sides of her heritage equally. When Selena was nine, her father formed a Tejano family band. Selena was the lead singer, her sister was the drummer, and her brother played bass guitar. Selena's father wrote most of the band's songs and the lyrics, which were all in Spanish. The band toured around Texas and released two Spanish language albums. When Selena was fifteen years old, she was named Female Entertainer of the Year at the 1986 Tejano Music Awards.

Selena and the band recorded more albums over the following years. At the 1994 Grammy Awards, Selena won Best Mexican American Album for her album *Selena Live*. She was the first Tejano singer to ever win in this category.

Selena was called the queen of Tejano music. With her husky voice and her energetic style of singing and dancing, she expanded the popularity of this music beyond Texas to all over the United States. Selena was also a fashion icon—she wore colorful and bold outfits onstage and even started her own clothing line. Most importantly, Selena broke down barriers for future Latina stars. Singer, actor, and dancer Jennifer Lopez (page 60) is so thankful she had Selena as a Latina role model.

"People like that don't come along every day," Jennifer said about her role model. "There's never going to be another Selena."

Selena was tragically killed in 1995 when she was twenty-three years old. A few months after her death, the studio released her only English language album, *Dreaming of You*. With this album, Selena became the first Latina solo artist to debut as number one on the Billboard 200. The album sold 175,000 copies on the first day of sales—this was a record for a female artist at the time.

"I feel that if you have a dream, don't let anybody take it away from you," Selena said. "And you always believe that the impossible is possible." Selena believed this, and we know some of her dreams did come true.

Shonda Rhimes

First Black Woman to Create and Produce a Major TV Series

BORN 1970

Shonda Rhimes is one of the most successful television producers ever. In 2005, she became the first Black woman to create and produce a major television series when she made *Grey's Anatomy* (TV-14), a show based around the lives of doctors and other medical staff at a Seattle, Washington, hospital. The show is one of the most popular shows in recent decades and has won four Emmy Awards.

When Shonda created *Grey's Anatomy*, it was very important to her that the cast be diverse. This was a first in the television industry at the time.

"We changed the faces that you see on television," Shonda said about her show. "And it should not have taken so long for that to happen."

In addition to *Grey's Anatomy*, Shonda has been a producer on several other popular TV shows, such as *Scandal* (TV-14) *Private Practice* (TV-14), and Bridgerton (TV-16) that have casts of people of different races and sexual orientations. Many of her lead actors also play well-developed Black female characters. Most writers and critics have described Shonda's characters as "smart and strong," but Shonda thinks that description should stop.

"Entertainment industry: time to stop using the phrases 'Smart Strong Women' and 'Strong Female Leads,'" Shonda tweeted. "There are no dumb weak women. A smart strong woman is just a WOMAN."

Shonda grew up outside Chicago. After graduating high school, she attended Dartmouth College and in 1991 earned an English and film studies degree. After graduation, Shonda moved to California to study screenwriting at the University of Southern California. In 2004, when she was thirty-five years old, Shonda wrote the screenplay for the movie *Princess Diaries 2: Royal Engagement*. *Grey's Anatomy* made its debut a year later.

Shonda has worked to get other women involved in broadcast by running a Women Directing Mentorship. She has also changed the people we see on television. She is proud of this, but she doesn't think it should be a big deal. It should just be the way it is. "I don't understand why people don't understand that the world of TV should look like the world outside of TV," Shonda said.

But more people are starting to see things Shonda's way, and TV is better for it.

Mickey Rowe

First Openly Autistic Actor to Play an Autistic Character Professionally

BORN 1988

When Mickey Rowe performed the lead role in *The Curious Incident of the Dog in the Night-Time*, he was doing nine performances a week. That is a lot—and one more than Broadway actors normally take on for a running show. Mickey wanted to prove he belonged on this stage and in this role—maybe belonged more than others.

Mickey was the first actor on the autism spectrum to perform the role of Christopher Boone professionally. Christopher Boone is an autistic character, but an actor on the autism spectrum had never been cast to play him. Mickey came along in 2017, five years after the show's first performance, and changed that.

"I think it's the theater's job to change the world," Mickey said. "I think it has a lot more power than it knows it has. And with that power comes great responsibility."

Mickey believes the theater world's great responsibility is to cast actors with disabilities in various roles but *especially* roles when the character is supposed to have disabilities. A high percentage of disabled roles are still filled by actors without disabilities. Mickey wants to change that.

"Disabled people are being excluded everywhere across the table," Mickey said. "I think entertainment is particularly important because inclusion in the arts really leads directly to inclusion in life."

Mickey grew up outside Seattle, Washington. He was not diagnosed with autism until college. He always knew there was something different about himself. He had trouble making friends and became obsessed with one activity or another. He attended the University of Washington and studied drama. While at the university, he finally learned he was on the spectrum when he went to a clinic that works with people with autism there. Mickey felt relieved. "You know your whole life that something is different," Mickey said. "You don't know why or what it is."

Once Mickey knew he was on the autism spectrum, he embraced the diagnosis. He wrote an essay on an entertainment industry website about his experience being an actor and being autistic. But it still hasn't been easy. Mickey struggles with making eye contact and picking up other people's emotional cues like anger or sadness. But he worked to overcome these barriers and continues to act in the theater. He also worked for other actors with disabilities to help them land similar opportunities.

"There is room for a multitude of perspectives," Mickey wrote. "Our differences are our strengths."

Lea Salonga

First Asian Woman to Win a Tony

BORN 1971

Until she was eighteen, this talented performer thought she would grow up to be Dr. Lea Salonga. She studied science in high school and was all set to start college and then go to medical school when her life changed almost overnight. Lea flew from the Philippines to London and New York City to become an international star, eventually becoming the first Asian female actor to win a coveted Tony Award.

Lea was born in the Philippines, where she loved singing for her family and friends. A cousin encouraged her to go to auditions, and Lea was soon a top child star. She even put out her first album when she was only nine! As a teenager, she appeared in movies, TV shows, and live performances, winning several national awards. All the time, however, she was still aiming at a medical career.

That changed when she was eighteen, when she won a key role in *Miss Saigon*, a musical set during the Vietnam War. She debuted in London, where her singing and acting talents thrilled audiences. The show soon moved to Broadway, and in 1991, Lea won the Tony Award for Best Leading Actress in a Musical, the first Asian performer to do so.

An even bigger barrier fell two years later when she became the first Asian female actor to take on the important role of a French girl named Éponine in the hit musical *Les Misérables*. Diverse casting of traditionally white roles was rare at the time, though that has improved in recent years. Lea has gone on to perform in more than a dozen other musicals and plays, winning awards in England, the United States, and her native country. Lea was also the singing voice of two famous Disney princesses: Jasmine in *Aladdin*, and the title character in *Mulan*. Lea's fans can also hear her on her many albums, where she has sung traditional American pop songs, other Broadway tunes, and traditional Filipino songs.

Throughout her long career, she has recognized the impact her success has had on other Asian and Asian American performers. "There are others who did come before me," she said. "I have to recognize there are shoulders that I'm standing on, and the chain continues, and there will be other Asian performers who will keep it going. It's like a really long relay race, and the baton keeps getting passed on."

TELEVISION ACTOR FILM ACTOR THEATER ACTOR MUSICIAN

Carol Shaw

First Woman to be a Professional Video Game Creator

BORN 1955

When Carol Shaw was a kid growing up in Palo Alto, California, she was really good at math. So good, in fact, she won a lot of local math awards and contests.

"Of course, people would say, 'Gee, you're good at math—for a girl,'" Carol explained. "That was kind of annoying. Why shouldn't girls be good at math?"

Carol's entire life involved leaping into spaces where most women had not yet gone...and then thriving. And she always liked building and creating things—especially train sets when she was a kid. In high school, Carol was the only girl playing text-based video games in the school's computer lab. Carol attended the University of California, Berkeley, and graduated with a degree in electrical engineering and computer science in 1977—one of the first women to graduate in this male-dominated field.

After graduation, Carol was hired by Atari. She had job offers from all over the country, but Atari was thrilled that they hired a female designer because they thought Carol would design simple color-matching games for them. Instead, Carol became one of the best programmers for their operating system at the time, the first professional female video game creator in the United States and, as one former coworker said, "one of the best programmers period."

Carol's first game was 3D tic-tac-toe for the Atari 2600. She designed it in 1980 when she was twenty-five years old. Three years later, Carol created a shooting game called *River Raid*. It became the eleventh-highest-selling Atari 2600 game ever and has sold more than 1.6 million copies.

Carol designed more games over the years, but she retired in 1990 at age thirty-five because of the money and investments she made from *River Raid*. She volunteered her time at the Foresight Institute, which researches emerging technologies. In 2017, the Games Awards gave Carol the Industry Icon Award. When she went to the stage to give her speech, female gamers and designers in the audience applauded loudly in appreciation. Carol had inspired the women in the audience as well as an entire generation of female computer scientists and video game designers to go after their dreams.

"People would say [video game design] is a white male-only arena," said Chris Garcia of the Computer History Museum. "Carol Shaw basically said they were wrong."

Ali Stroker

First Wheelchair-Using Actor to Win a Tony

BORN 1987

When Ali Stroker was a little girl, she looked around for people like her who were achieving their dreams. But she "never saw anyone in a wheelchair going after what they wanted," she said.

So, Ali decided when she grew up, she would change that—and she did. In 2019, at age thirty-two, Ali became the first Broadway actor who uses a wheelchair to win a Tony Award. The award was for her role as Ado Annie in the musical *Oklahoma*. In Ali's acceptance speech at the award ceremony, she said, "This award is for every kid who is watching tonight who has a disability, who has a limitation or a challenge, who has been waiting to see themselves represented in this arena. You [now] are."

Ali grew up in Ridgewood, New Jersey. When she was two years old, she was in a car accident that left her paralyzed from the chest down. She can't even remember walking, but she can remember the color of her first wheelchair. It was bright red.

When Ali was seven, a twelve-year-old neighborhood friend told her that she was going to direct a backyard version of the musical *Annie*. The neighbor cast Ali in the lead role. Ali loved this first experience, and it set her acting and singing career in motion. The one thing that Ali discovered she really liked about performing was the power that came with it. As a person who uses a wheelchair, strangers sometimes stared at Ali whether she wanted them to or not. But when she was on the stage, she was the one in control. She asked people to watch her.

"As an artist, I'm saying, 'Look at me now. Look at my body. Look how I move my chair,'" Ali explained. "I'm asking, and that makes me feel my most powerful self."

Ali was her class president at Ridgewood High School and also starred in the school's musicals. After high school, she attended New York University. In 2009, she became the first graduate who uses a wheelchair from the Tisch School of the Arts drama program. Her breakout role came six years later when she was cast in a revival of the show *Spring Awakening*. In that role, she was the first actor who uses a wheelchair to appear on Broadway. She has appeared in many television shows including *Glee* and *Only Murders in the Building*.

Ali is an ambassador for the American Association of People with Disabilities. But what she really wants is to advocate for kids like her who also want to act and perform. She has one message for them: "You can do it!"

Wes Studi

First Indigenous American Oscar Winner

BORN 1947

For decades, Indigenous characters in most American movies were not played by Indigenous people. That has very much begun to change, and Wes Studi's success is a key reason. The groundbreaking Cherokee actor has had a long and celebrated career, becoming the first Indigenous American to win an Oscar.

Wes was born in Oklahoma and spoke only Cherokee until he was five. For a while, his family lived on a ranch with few Indigenous people around. That changed when he went to a high school with lots of Indigenous kids. After school, Wes joined the U.S. Army and served in the Vietnam War. Because of the frightening experiences he had in combat, Wes tried to spread peace when he came back. That led to working in the early 1970s in the American Indian Movement, a group that called for rights and equality for Indigenous people.

Wes was in his early forties and working for the Cherokee Nation as a writer and teacher before he found acting. After landing a few roles in Oklahoma, he moved to Los Angeles, where he got his big break playing a Pawnee warrior in 1990's *Dances with Wolves* (PG-13). The movie was a huge hit, winning Oscars and worldwide acclaim. Wes later starred in *Geronimo: An American Legend* (PG-13), where he was the Apache leader. Wes has played roles as many different Indigenous people and even learned new languages to fully understand the roles. He has taken on many non-Indigenous roles as well, such as in *Avatar* (PG-13).

Indigenous actors and others look at Wes as an inspiration and trailblazer. Seminole and Muscogee writer and producer Sterlin Harjo said, "[Wes] laid the groundwork for a lot of the stuff that people are doing now. [There are more] contemporary roles. It's not 'We're going to make a Hollywood Western with cowboys and Indians.'"

In 2019, Wes's career and influence were recognized when he became the first Indigenous American actor to receive an Oscar: it was the Governors Award, given to people for a career of achievement in the movies. Wes continues acting today while also sharing his talents as an author, musician, and artist specializing in carving. In 2024, he performed as Attakullakulla, his real-life ancestor, in a Cherokee history play, *Nanyehi—The Story of Nancy Ward.*

ARTIST

MUSICIAN

AUTHOR

FILM ACTOR

Taylor Swift

First Musician to Generate $1 Billion from a Concert Tour

BORN 1989

On March 17, 2023, Taylor Swift walked onstage in Glendale, Arizona, to kick off her epic Eras tour. Wearing a blue, pink, and purple gemmed bodysuit, Taylor performed in front of a crowd of more than 69,000 people—the largest audience for a female performer in United States history. Nine months later, she was named the *Time* magazine Person of the Year, the first person to be recognized for this honor for their work in the arts.

In 2023 and 2024, Taylor performed over 150 shows on five continents, and the Eras tour became the highest grossing concert tour of all time and the first to ever earn over a billion dollars (Over four billion in fact!). The tour was earth shaking—for real. At a show in Seattle Washington, Taylor's dancing fans generated a 2.3-magnitude earthquake, named *Swiftquake*. Taylor soon brought the concert tour to the big screen, where it became the highest grossing U.S. concert film of all time.

Taylor is a fearless first in every sense. Throughout her career she has constantly evolved and challenged norms, while also making the world a better place through her music.

"To me fearless isn't not having fears, it's not that you're not afraid of anything," Taylor said. "I think that being fearless is having a lot of fears, but you jump anyway."

Taylor leaped into the musical industry from a very young age. She grew up on a Christmas tree farm in Reading, Pennsylvania, with her dad, mom, and brother. She started performing at twelve, and when she was fourteen, her family moved to Tennessee so she could explore a country music career. Her first self-titled album was released in 2006, when Taylor was seventeen.

Taylor transitioned from country to pop music seamlessly, generating new fans with every new album. In the seventeen years since her first album, Taylor has made more number one albums than any other women in history. In 2023 alone, she had three. Through her music and song writing, Taylor is the ultimate storyteller, and everybody wants to hear what she has to say. This is especially meaningful because Taylor is an advocate for positive change—she has championed LGBTQIA+ rights, spoken up for women who faced harassment, and encouraged people to vote.

"You should celebrate who you are now, where you're going, and where you've been," she said.

Taylor celebrates this message through her songs, and the world is grateful for it.

Maria Tallchief

First Indigenous American Prima Ballerina for a Major American Ballet Company

1925–2013

When Maria Tallchief first began her career, it was common for American dancers to adopt Russian stage names. (Stage names are what a person goes by professionally.) Dancers were taking Russian-sounding names because Russian ballet was considered the best at the time. Maria refused. "Never!" she told anybody who tried to persuade her. Maria was proud of her Osage Nation heritage. She decided she wanted to stand out, not fit in.

Maria did just that. When she was twenty-two years old, she became America's first Indigenous major prima ballerina as a dancer in the New York City Ballet. The label of *prima ballerina* meant she was the best dancer onstage.

Maria was born in Fairfax, Oklahoma, on the Osage Reservation. Her father was Osage, and her mother was of Scottish and Irish descent. Maria went to powwows—Indigenous American gatherings where people danced to the beat of a drum—when she was growing up. It was there that she fell in love with dancing.

When Maria was eight, her family moved off their reservation and bought a home in Los Angeles, California. Maria began taking ballet lessons. The lessons were wonderful. But living in Los Angeles was the first time she was surrounded by people who weren't Indigenous American like her.

"[Some kids] made war whoops whenever they saw me and asked why I didn't wear feathers or if my father took scalps," Maria said. "The experience was painful."

When Maria danced, it helped her escape this racism. She danced all the way through high school. When she graduated in 1942, she moved across the country to New York City to become a professional ballerina. At age twenty-two, she was named the prima ballerina of the New York City Ballet.

Maria danced for eighteen more years. She danced with power, grace, and, most importantly, emotion.

"Dance is not just a physical activity. It's a spiritual one as well," Maria said.

Maria was not just the first Indigenous American prima ballerina in the United States. She was also one of the best dancers to have ever danced and is considered the first *major* prima ballerina of any ethnicity in the U.S. She received many awards and honors throughout her career. But one that was most important to her was when she was given the name Wa-Xthe Thomba when she was twenty-eight years old. This name she wore proudly. It means *Woman of Two Worlds.*

Cicely Tyson

First Black Star of a TV Drama

1924–2021

If there was a way to perform, Cicely Tyson found it and conquered it, no matter what obstacles were in her way. Her seventy-year career in entertainment was filled with firsts and honors from her work in TV, movies, and on the stage. She was the first Black woman to star in a TV drama. She acted in more than one hundred television, movie, and theater roles and won numerous awards and honors. Through it all, Cicely insisted that the Black characters she played be presented with dignity. She refused to take roles that portrayed Black people as criminals or as bad people and encouraged other Black actors to do the same.

"I want to be recalled as one who squared my shoulders in the service of Black women," Cicely said, "as one who made us walk taller and envision greater for ourselves."

Cicely grew up in East Harlem, New York. After she graduated high school in 1942, she became a fashion model. In her work as a model, Cicely helped influence Black fashion and hairstyles. She was among the first Black models to wear her hair in a natural Afro style in photos, for example. By the 1950s, she was also acting onstage and on TV. In 1963, Cicely became the first Black regular member of a TV show cast, in the series *East Side/West Side*. Even better, she played a professional in an office, which a Black woman had never done before. By the end of the decade, she was a movie star too. In 1972, she earned an Oscar nomination for her role in the movie *Sounder*.

A highlight of her long career came in 2003, when she earned the first of her three career Emmy Awards for playing a 110-year-old formerly enslaved woman telling the story of her life in *The Autobiography of Miss Jane Pittman*.

In 2013, when she was eighty-eight, she won a Tony Award for her work in the play *A Trip to Bountiful*. At the time, she was the oldest person ever to win that important award for drama. For her work in entertainment and activism, President Barack Obama gave her the Presidential Medal of Freedom in 2016. In 2018, she added another trophy to her shelves; she became the first Black female actor to be given an honorary Oscar for career achievement. As an actor and a role model for Black women, Cicely was an entertainment icon.

Oprah Winfrey

Richest Black Woman in the United States

BORN 1954

When Oprah Winfrey was twenty-four years old in 1978, she made her first appearance as a television talk show host. "This is what I was born to do," Oprah said.

Fast-forward more than forty years since Oprah's debut, and she is now one of the most famous, successful, and powerful people in the world. She is a talk show host, executive, actor, and one of the first Black female billionaires in the United States.

Oprah was born in Kosciusko, Mississippi. From an early age, she loved to talk. At only three years old, she recited Bible passages at her church services. When Oprah was eight, she moved to Nashville, Tennessee. In 1971, when Oprah was seventeen, she entered a Miss Teen Fire Prevention Pageant where she told the judges that she wanted to be a journalist on television one day. So, a local radio station called Oprah and asked if she wanted to read the news on the air for them. Oprah was so good at it that a television news station in Nashville then asked her to be an on-air reporter. Oprah became the first Black female news anchor in Nashville history.

Three years later, when Oprah was twenty-two, she became a television news anchor in Baltimore, Maryland. Oprah had a lot of warmth and personality on the air. So much so that a producer thought Oprah would be better as a talk show host than a news reporter. So, Oprah began to cohost a show called *People Are Talking*. This cohosting gig helped Oprah land her own show, *The Oprah Winfrey Show*, based in Chicago, when she was just thirty-two years old. That same year, Oprah started her own production company, Harpo Studios. (It is her name spelled backward.)

The Oprah Winfrey Show was a hit. Viewers loved how honest and kind Oprah was. Her show ran for twenty-five seasons and became the highest-rated talk show in American television history.

Thanks to Oprah's production company, she has made so much money from her show, her own cable channel, her magazine, and on other movies and shows she produced. She has also acted in movies like *The Color Purple* and *A Wrinkle in Time*. Oprah used a lot of her earnings to help other people, especially children and women. She even opened a boarding school for girls in South Africa.

In 2018, Oprah became the first Black woman to win a Golden Globe Lifetime Achievement Award. "Speaking your truth is the most powerful tool we all have," Oprah said in her acceptance speech. By 2023, because of her continued successes in her business endeavors, she was one of the richest Black women on the planet.

Anna May Wong

First Asian American Movie Star

1905–1961

In the early days of Hollywood, almost all the actors were white, even though some of the films were set in Asia or had Asian characters. The first Asian American actor to break through with big parts was Anna May Wong. But even as her stardom grew, she was kept from playing positive roles and was usually cast as a villain. She pushed back against such stereotypes and helped blaze a trail for Asian American actors of the future.

Anna May was born Wong Liu Tsong in Los Angeles. Her parents, who were from China, ran a laundromat, where Anna May would help after school. But she also spent time visiting movie sets in LA, the center of the moviemaking business. She got parts as an extra in her teens and landed larger roles by the early 1920s. However, she was frustrated by only getting stereotyped roles as maids or servants.

Anna May moved to Europe to find more opportunities and appeared in several movies and plays there. Returning to the United States in the early 1930s, she got her most famous role in *Shanghai Express*. Of course, it was for one of the "bad" people in the film.

"I was so tired of the parts I had to play," she said. "Why is it that the Chinese [role] is nearly always the villain of the piece? How [can that be], with a civilization that's so many times older than that of the West?"

She was even turned down for the lead role in *The Good Earth*, a movie set entirely in China—the role went to a white actor—and she couldn't play a romantic role. There were actually laws against showing interracial kisses in movies!

Anna May kept fighting and acting, however, working in the United States, China, and Europe for many years. She retired in the early 1940s but returned to acting in 1951 when she starred in a TV show, *The Gallery of Madame Liu-Tsong*. That made her the first Asian American TV star as well.

Anna May died in 1961 in Los Angeles. Since then, her reputation has grown, and many actors today point to her as an inspiration. In 2023, she was honored again by becoming the first Asian American to be pictured on U.S. money when her portrait was part of the American Women Quarters program from the U.S. Mint.

Michelle Yeoh

First Asian Woman to Win Best Actress Oscar

BORN 1962

Michelle Yeoh has been known for her awesome martial arts skills, fighting robbers, spies, mummies, and more in films for over forty years. But she did not win Best Actress at the Academy Awards until 2023, and she was the first Asian person to ever win in the category.

Michelle was born Yeoh Choo Kheng in Malaysia. Her parents were from China. When she was young, she enjoyed many sports, including squash and swimming; she also studied ballet for many years. In fact, she moved to England to study dance and attend college. While she was there, her mother entered her into a beauty pageant back home. When Michelle returned for vacation, she was surprised at having been entered, but she finished the pageant as the winner and became Miss Malaysia! Her fame led to her work acting in commercials and soon in movies. She moved to Hong Kong, a major center of Asian films.

Michelle's athletic skills helped her become a star in action movies, for which she learned martial arts and how to do stunts. Her early movies were in Chinese, but Michelle soon earned key parts in English-language movies too. In 2000, she starred in the Chinese-language *Crouching Tiger, Hidden Dragon* (PG-13), which became a hit around the world. Michelle's work in the film included leaping and soaring over buildings. Still, being an action star was becoming harder to do as she got older, especially as she had suffered several injuries doing the stunts.

Michelle has done voice acting in films such as *Kung Fu Panda 2* and *Minions: The Rise of Gru*. She's also played multiple characters in Marvel films, including *Guardians of the Galaxy Vol. 2* (PG-13) and *Shang-Chi and the Legend of the Ten Rings* (PG-13). A starring role in the very popular *Crazy Rich Asians* (PG-13) in 2017 earned her a lot of praise. And in 2022, at the age of sixty, Michelle performed the role that earned her the Oscar in *Everything, Everywhere, All at Once* (R), showing off both her action skills and her ability to play several characters. It was a breakout year for Asian actors, four of whom were nominated for Academy Awards.

In her acceptance speech, she said, "For all the little boys and girls who look like me watching tonight, this is a beacon of hope and possibility. And ladies, don't let anyone ever tell you [that] you are past your prime."

ENTERTAINERS THROUGH THE YEARS

1811
The magician Richard Potter draws crowds to American theaters.

1876
Edmonia Lewis's sculpture *The Death of Cleopatra* is put on display in Philadelphia.

1919
Oscar Micheaux debuts his film *The Homesteader*.

1932
Anna May Wong performs in her most famous movie, *The Shanghai Express*.

1939
Marian Anderson performs a concert at Lincoln Memorial.

1939
Hattie McDaniel wins an Oscar for Best Supporting Actress.

1947
Maria Tallchief is named Major Prima Ballerina in the New York City Ballet.

1950
Juanita Hall wins a Tony Award for *South Pacific*.

1951
Lucille Ball and Desi Arnaz create *I Love Lucy*.

1956
Nat King Cole hosts his own television show.

1956
James Wong Howe wins an Oscar for Best Cinematography.

1964
Joanne Funakoshi debuts with the Ice Capades.

1965
The East West Players theater opens in Los Angeles.

1977
Ashley Boone Jr. green-lights *Star Wars* as a movie executive.

1977
Rita Moreno wins an Emmy, completing her EGOT.

1977
Carol Shaw is hired as a video game creator at Atari.

1980
Larry Hama creates a new comic book series about G.I. Joe.

1980
Geri Jewell appears on *The Facts of Life*.

1982
Quincy Jones produces *Thriller*, the best-selling album of all time.

1986
Coco Mitchell appears in *Sports Illustrated*.

1987
Aretha Franklin is inducted into the Rock & Roll Hall of Fame.

1987
Marlee Matlin wins an Oscar for Best Actress.

1989
Chris Burke stars in *Life Goes On*.

1991
Lea Salonga wins a Tony for *Miss Saigon*.

1994
Toni Morrison wins the Nobel Prize for Literature.

1995
Selena Quintanilla's solo artist album debuts as No. 1.

2001
Jennifer Lopez has a No. 1 album and No. 1 movie in the same week.

2003
Oprah Winfrey becomes a billionaire.

2005
Shonda Rhimes creates and produces *Grey's Anatomy*.

2008 Matthew López wins the Tony Award for Best Play.

2011 Peter Dinklage wins an Emmy for acting in *Game of Thrones*.

2012 Laverne Cox wins a Daytime Emmy Award.

2013 At age eighty-eight, Cicely Tyson wins a Tony Award.

2015 Juan Felipe Herrera is named U.S. poet laureate.

2010 Children's book illustrator Jerry Pinkney wins the Caldecott Medal.

2012 Mindy Kaling creates, writes, and stars in *The Mindy Project*.

2013 Cornbread is inducted into the Graffiti Hall of Fame in New York City.

2015 Misty Copeland becomes the principal dancer at the American Ballet Theatre.

2016 Alexandra Kutas models at New York Fashion Week.

2017 Mahershala Ali wins an Oscar for Best Actor.

2017 Model Ashley Graham appears on the cover of *Vogue*.

2019 Patricia Cardoso's film *Real Women Have Curves* is added to National Film Registry.

2016 Viet Thanh Nguyen wins the Pulitzer Prize for Fiction.

2017 Amanda Gorman is named the National Youth Poet Laureate.

2017 Mickey Rowe is the lead in *The Curious Incident of the Dog in the Nighttime*.

2019 Ruth E. Carter wins her first Oscar for Best Costume Design.

2019 Billy Porter wins an Emmy Award for Lead Actor in a Drama.

2019 Wes Studi wins an Oscar for his career achievements.

2021 Sierra Teller Ornelas is named showrunner of *Rutherford Falls*.

2023 Michelle Yeoh wins an Oscar for Best Actress.

2019 Actress Ali Stoker wins a Tony Award for *Oklahoma*.

2020 Billie Eilish wins four Grammy Awards.

2021 Megan Piphus Peace becomes a full-time puppeteer on *Sesame Street*.

2023 Taylor Swift begins the Eras tour, the first tour to generate over one billion dollars.

ROLL
SCENE
TAKE
SOUND
DATE
PROD. CO
DIRECTOR
CAMERAMAN

Find Out More!

Check out these books to discover more about some of the entertainers mentioned in this book and learn about others who broke barriers and made history!

Carter, Ruth E. *The Art of Ruth E. Carter: Costuming Black History and the Afrofuture, from Do the Right Thing to Black Panther.* San Francisco: Chronicle Books, 2023.

Copeland, Misty. *Life in Motion: An Unlikely Ballerina Young Reader's Edition*. New York: Aladdin, 2016.

Day, Christine and Chelsea Clinton. *She Persisted: Maria Tallchief*. New York: Philomel Books, 2021

Etinde-Crompton, Charlotte. *Edmonia Lewis: Internationally Renowned Sculptor (Celebrating Black Artists)*. Minneapolis: Enslow Publishers, 2019.

Denise, Anika Aldamuy. *A Girl Named Rosita: The Story of Rita Moreno, Actor, Singer, Dancer, Trailblazer!* New York: HarperCollins, 2020.

Favilli, Elena and Francesca Cavallo. *Goodnight Stories For Rebel Girls*. San Francisco, Rebel Girls, 2016.

Gorman, Amanda and Loren Long. *Change Sings: A Children's Anthem*. New York: Viking Books, 2021.

Herrera, Juan Felipe. *Imagine*. Boston: Candlewick, 2021.

Herrera, Juan Felipe. *Portraits of Hispanic American Heroes*. New York: Dial Books, 2014.

Kramer, Barbara. *Who Is Oprah Winfrey?* New York: Penguin Workshop, 2019.

Medina, Nico. *Who Was Aretha Franklin?* New York: Penguin Workshop, 2018.

Russell-Brown, Katheryn and Chelsea Clinton. *She Persisted: Marian Anderson*. New York: Philomel Books, 2022.

Pollack, Pam. *Who Was Lucille Ball?* New York: Penguin Workshop, 2017.

Smith, Elliott. *Black Achievement in Entertainment: Celebrating Hattie McDaniel, Chadwick Boseman, and More*. Minneapolis: Lerner Publications, 2023.

Stroker, Ali. *Ali and the Sea Stars*. New York: HarperCollins, 2022.

Thanh Nguyen, Viet. *Chicken of the Sea*. New York: McSweeneys, 2019.

Vegara, Maria Isabel Sanchez. *Laverne Cox (Little People, BIG DREAMS)*. London, England: Frances Lincoln Children's Books, 2022.

Wolf, Analiza and Bryson Wolf. *Native Americans Who Inspire Us*. Self-published, 2022.

Yoo, Paula. *Shining Star: The Anna May Wong Story*. New York: Lee & Low, 2016.

A Message from the Authors

We hope you enjoyed reading about these fearless firsts in the entertainment industry. These individuals are a testament to what can be achieved through determination, will power, and grit. These trailblazing actors, musicians, writers, and more have opened doors for future generations. They toppled prejudices and knocked down discrimination walls to make the entertainment industry a more welcoming and accepting place for all.

Yet, it's still important to remember there are more fearless firsts to be discovered. The industry is always evolving and with that comes fresh chances to break new ground and overcome barriers. What visionary performer will be discovered next? We want to make sure we don't miss them. This is why we wanted to ask you, our readers, for help. Keep your eyes and ears open to seek out new trailblazers. Everybody deserves a chance to achieve their dream — especially you. The future of entertainment is bright: It will only get brighter if more diverse performers are given the opportunity to shine their light in the years to come.

About the Authors

Photo © Patty Kelley

James Buckley Jr. is one of the country's most prolific writers of nonfiction books for kids, with more than two hundred titles to his name on dozens of topics. He has written twenty-five books in the *New York Times*–bestselling Who Was...? biography series and nine books in the Show Me History graphic nonfiction series. James has recounted the lives of everyone from Muhammad Ali, Gandhi, and Amelia Earhart to Blackbeard, Betsy Ross, and the Wright brothers.

A former editor with *Sports Illustrated* and NFL Publishing, James runs Shoreline Publishing Group, a leading producer of nonfiction kids' books for national and school-library publishers. Shoreline has produced books about moviemaking, creating comic books, celebrity biographies, fashion design, and many other topics. He lives in Santa Barbara, California, where he is the coproducer of the local production of Bloomsday, an annual salute to Irish author James Joyce.

Photo © Jeff Labrecque

Ellen Labrecque loves sharing stories about entertainers who dare to be first. She hopes these tales inspire the next generation of storytellers, actors, and artists to fearlessly pursue their own dreams. Ellen has authored more than one hundred nonfiction children's books. She has written thirteen biographies in the *New York Times* bestselling Who Was...? series, including singer and actor Frank Sinatra and poet and author Maya Angelou.

Ellen lives in Bucks County, Pennsylvania, with a family of movie buffs and Broadway enthusiasts. An avid reader herself, Ellen may be one of the only people you'll ever meet who proudly wears a T-shirt espousing the glories of the Oxford comma.